Dørkiſmø

Dørkišmø

The macho of the dork

Maria Bustillos

Please visit the website at www.dorkismo.com

ISBN-13: 978-0-615-25617-7

Book design by Marie Mundaca.

Printed in the United States of America

First Printing: August 2009

For Carmen and Oliver, my favorite dorks,
and in memory of David Wallace

Contents

Esse quam videri — Cicero

Tǒ +hiπe øwπ ſeℓ̧ſ 6e cøø¹

(øπe.)

I once attended this uppity little liberal-arts college where they held the usual film screenings every Friday night. Desperate to become an intellectual, which in those days meant learning French (especially phrases like *film noir*) and knowing all about European art and movies, I never missed these events and indeed, quickly learned to stop saying "movie," ever, and I would not put it past me even to have worn a beret, because I had bought one in Paris the summer before school started. So one night they showed *The Seventh Seal,* which is a really good movie, or film, despite its intimidatingly high reputation, and everyone sobbed buckets because the ending is so sad. The lights went up, and all of us Europeanized junior sophisticates were red-eyed and stricken-looking, and I felt so strongly that we were sharing the same powerful sensations of futility, and sadness, with a bleak, bleached-out bit of Scandinavian hope thrown in. It was a confederacy of deep-thinking, deep-feeling young people, who cared about truth and beauty and the life of the mind, and so forth! I was dazzled. How I wanted to be here, to be part of this. For them to think I was as detached and sardonic and not-quite-American as they. Probably I lit a cigarette, and readjusted my beret at a more serious angle.

A week or two later we got to see *The Great Dictator,* the Charlie Chaplin classic in which a timid little Jewish barber who happens to look exactly like the dictator Adenoid Hynkel eventually seizes his chance to address the assembled armies of Tomania in the most stirring, beautiful, sentimental speech you could ever imagine. Chaplin's quivering face fills the whole screen as he shouts things like: "Let us fight for a world of reason, a world where science and progress will lead to all men's happiness. Soldiers, in the name of democracy, let us all unite!"

I was seeing this movie for the first time, and sobbed buckets again. But when the lights came up this time I found, to my horror, that I was the only red-eyed customer. My sophisticated comrades had scorned to cry at such schmaltz and now commenced, with varying degrees of tolerant eye-rolling, to mock my low tastes.

For a teenager, embarrassment is scarcely distinguishable from disembowelment; for a minute I really wanted to disown the film, to downplay how much I had loved it; to drawl, "God I know, I'm such a fool, I will cry at the stupidest thing," true as that is. But I couldn't find it in me to betray the emotion the movie had evoked, nor my admiration for Chaplin's genius; no, not even to be admitted back into the bosom of the intellectuals. So I kind of broke with those guys a little bit, right then; in one way terrified, but in another, with a strange feeling that it was they, not I, who had strayed from our once-connected path. Because why should anyone be embarrassed to love Charlie Chaplin? Isn't Chaplin as worthy as or even worthier than Bergman, who is kind of bereft of all but the blackest humor? Isn't it bizarre, and brave and even sublime, right in the middle of a war, to conflate a fruity, slapstick *pas de deux avec* a balloon with the terrors of fascism? Wasn't the emotional range of *The Great Dictator* (made in 1940!) far more complicated, more compelling, more intellectually demanding, even, than that of *The Seventh Seal?* Hell yes, I thought. If that makes me a yahoo, or whatever, so be it; I could go only so far to obtain the high-groove approval. Thus and thus, in my own life, the first slight stirrings of dorkismo began, though it would be years before I would muster up the courage not just to admit under duress, but to announce breezily right up front that Edward Lear is my favorite poet, that I love *Star Wars,* iceberg lettuce, Benny Hill, etc. etc.

Of course we all are dorks, deep down inside. Dorkismo is not about just being okay with that. Rather, dorkismo is the capacity for opening up and reveling in your own dork nature. By "dork," I should say, I mean the nuance common-

2. Dork

Someone who has odd interests, and is often silly at times. A dork is also someone who can be themselves and not care what anyone thinks.

You are such a dork.

Source: Blah, Nov 19, 2003

101 up, 22 down
click to vote

link
send
redefine
remove
be an editor

ly but not exclusively ascribed to this slang word, the first of the three definitions given below (courtesy of urbandictionary.com)[1]

1. A person who "can be themselves and not care what anyone thinks."

2. A socially inept or clumsy person (but essentially, a variant of (1), because indicative of willingness to attempt activities in public at which the subject does not excel.)

3. Someone who is into computers, engineering and/or role-playing games, sci-fi/fantasy literature and stuff like that (but in practice, another variant of (1), because an obvious dedication to "uncool" pursuits such as these almost guarantees ridicule and/or ostracism.)

URBANdictionary.com Look up: dork search

B C D E F G H I J K L M N O P Q R S T U V W X Y Z

new def | daily email | random | be an editor | store

17. Dork

click to vote

link
send
redefine
remove
be an editor

Someone that, no matter how many disses they get from people in this room making definitions of them, are actually getting more chicks then everyone these days. And let's face it people, we're all dorks inside. We all want to be ourselves but we can't. But it seems like we don't even know what to consider a dork nowadays. So let's just call all the losers nerds or geeks...or better yet losers.

Jock #1: Dude, we can't let those dork fags take our girls. it's like a freaking dork revolution!

Jock #2: I know man. We can't let them. So let's just continue to get other chicks who are hotter and make them jealous.

Cool Jock: Like who else? All the actually hot and cool chicks are gone. I mean, their's always a couple of really hot chicks but they're all sluts/ dumbasses/ so not fun...

Random Faggish kid whose popular because of a corrupted society: Fuck that shit dude...i just wanna get wasted again

Cool Jock: You do that....I'm gonna go hang out with some of those dudes.

All the jocks: But they're like....

Cool Jock: Cool and not corrupted and really dumbasses like most of us? I know. Later.

Source: Xtreme Christ, Mar 31, 2005

Like its etymological prototype, "machismo," dorkismo connotes a kind of inner pride and self-confidence. It is the Macho of the Dork, or dork *cojones*, if you like: the courage to be yourself, despite the risk or even certainty of being thought a total idiot. You might stick to your guns in the face of ostracism cheerfully, or defensively, or shyly. But if you do stick to them, you can't help but stop caring so much what other people think. Your dorkismo bulletproofs you. Eventually, outside influences lose their power to compel or frighten you into doing much of anything at all.

Conversely, anyone with dorkismo is liable to treat others with an affable open-mindedness, because who cares if anyone else agrees with you or not in the matter of wine, movies or political candidates. It's okay! You could like them anyway. Offering freely the tolerance you hope will be extended to your own peculiarities, you are at liberty to investigate the ways of others in a brotherly, inclusive spirit.

(Ťwǿ.)

The desire to fit in and the desire to break free of the herd are forever at war in the human breast. Some people are in a perpetual tizz about what others think or might think of them; the yes-men, the suckers, the hipsters, or at their worst, those Eichmann-like tools of authority, obediently yanking the lever for Dr. Milgram. Then there are the reactionaries (punks, anarchists, religious fanatics *et al.*) whose every move is in reflex opposition to what they imagine *hoi polloi* are up to; they're just like yes-men, but backwards (no-men, I guess.) At the other end of the spectrum, we find the alienated individual who is completely absorbed in himself alone, unconcerned about anyone *but* himself; this kind of consummately inner-directed, nonconformist personality is more commonly known as a "sociopath."

Fortunately most of us, being dorks, fall somewhere in the middle of this spectrum. We're reasonably concerned about other people, and we desire their companionship, approval, friendship and trust. To that extent, we're conformists. We also have our own aims entirely distinct from everyone else's, and deep personal beliefs that no one can alter. By balancing these opposing forces we manage to belong to our families, communities and culture, but without losing an essential sense of self. This balance is self-evidently required for wholeness, happiness and sanity. It also ensures that people are going to find you a little weird, because dorks don't always conform, nor do they always rebel; sometimes they can—or they must—"be themselves and not care what anyone thinks."

You may think all that is kind of trivial, but consider how valuable a weapon a resiliently dorky self-possession can be against such oppressive forces as a cruel and mendacious government, or a blind, greedy corpocracy, or against religious extremism and intolerance. The forces of oppression are actually *counting on* and *exploiting* our fear of not fitting in. A general waking-up from the anesthesia of conformist cultural pressures might well empower not only individuals, but a whole society against threats to liberty such as these.

Being a big dork is something that George Orwell never explicitly conceived of as the ideal way to fight Big Brother, and yet here was a practical solution to the problem of institutionalized coercion, right under his own nose. Or in his own heart, I should say, because Orwell was a world-class dork himself, as evidenced, among many other things, by the brilliant apologia he wrote on behalf of the low culture of his times. For example, his essay "Good Bad Books" matily encourages all comers to enjoy trashy literature:

> All one can say is that, while civilisation remains such that one needs distraction from time to time, "light" literature has its appointed place; also that there is such a thing as sheer skill, or native grace, which may have more survival value than erudition or intellectual power. There are music-hall songs which are better poems than three-quarters of the stuff that gets into the anthologies:
>
> > *Come where the booze is cheaper,*
> > *Come where the pots hold more,*
> > *Come where the boss is a bit of a sport,*
> > *Come to the pub next door!* [2]

(Three.)

We have come to take the miracle of *flying in the air* for granted. Air travel is something to be endured as blindly as possible, either asleep or zoned out in front of the laptop. Also you're supposed to be acting all cool and blasé as you *blast your way through the sky in a 200-ton metal cylinder with wings,* maybe, so that nobody thinks that you are some kind of a rube who has never been on an airplane. But there was a glorious exception to the general ennui just recently, one of many inspirations for this book: a long-haired wag in his mid-twenties, seated behind us on a flight to JFK, setting forth on what was obviously a long-anticipated holiday with a few agreeably rowdy friends. Just as the plane took off, in that weird weightless-yet-super-heavy moment, the wings tilting up, over the boiling thunder of the engines he roared, "ENGAGE!" and we were vaulted into the heavens.

The freedom to shriek on takeoff, for fun, if you want to! This is dorkismo.

Pity by contrast the poor avant-gardist, trapped in a permanent state of bilious disapproval, straitjacketed into his world of safe little hatreds. Nothing surprises, excites or delights him. His world-weariness has slowly eaten up his whole personality until he cannot dare to admire so much as a pair of tennis shoes, for fear they might be the wrong kind. He never permits himself to say, "Wow!" anymore, let alone shriek "ENGAGE!", or anything else, on an airplane.

I know one such guy, it pains me to say, a high-school junior. Jaded sixteen-year-olds are the merest cliché, I guess, but it is still pretty sad. David is a gorgeous, slender, sloe-eyed, delightfully lazy-looking creature, highly intelligent and a musical prodigy besides, which facts have got all his comrades in total awe of him, a position of superiority he exploits to the utmost degree. This paragon was recently heard to announce, "It's not cool anymore to like Of Montreal." Two or three of the others chimed in nervously, "Oh yeah, I'm so over them," and things like that. And so, Of Montreal (of whom I am very fond, which made this whole episode particularly vexing) are in the doghouse with a whole high-school's worth of kids, until maybe David should decide they are okay again.

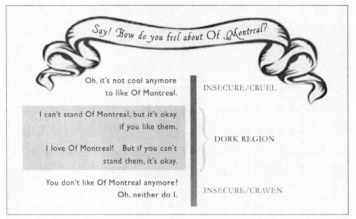

Fig. 1., Of Montreal Coercion-Gradient.

Notice he did not say, "Of Montreal sucks," "Dude looks like a fag in that dress" or anything like that, just "it's not cool anymore" to like them. He made no argument; he merely commanded, exercising his power out of pure caprice, for the pleasure of it; lording it over his friends, a fiendishly attractive agent of negativity and repression (see Fig. 1., Of Montreal Coercion-Gradient.)

As illustrated above, it is *liberty* that the dorks are really after; for themselves, and for everybody else. But in today's America, the delicate tension required for maximum liberty has been knocked out of whack. Too many of us are chasing the approval and the status and the money too hard, or else trying to set ourselves up as unimpeachable authorities, in a way that tends to make us all ever more insecure, shallow, closed-minded and materialistic. Sadder still, the approval and the money and the status do not fix us, not even when we have got a lot of those; the unfortunate tendency is to suppose that that is only because we haven't got quite enough yet, and we need to go chase some more. A lot of very good books have been written about how unhealthy and distressing all that is, from *Luxury Fever* to *Status Anxiety*, but none of them (until now!) has offered a credible way out. Not credible, because not sensible, and not fun. We have been scolded and berated and informed that we need to become more involved politically, read more philosophy, trim our materialistic desires and vandalize shopping-cart machines (more on all of which anon,) but none of these suggestions is at all likely to change a single person's course. The big dorks are the only ones showing us the way off the hamster wheel, and it's the way we wanted to go all along. It's not just that a little nonconformity is healthy, and a lot of fun; it's that human beings need some detachment in order to negotiate our own sanity. This book was written in order to make the case for dorkismo, a readily available, already plentiful, free and obvious means of taking back our personal freedom in a way that makes sense, is fun, and will promote happiness.

So I'm not going to tell you how to be backwardsly cool, by giving you techniques that would make people consider you a dork, and therefore very cool, though I don't doubt some fool is going on that fool's errand soon. The trend forecaster Irma Zandl said in *Time* magazine: " 'I'm working on a theory right now that I haven't really fully fleshed out,' she says cautiously. 'I'm calling it "The Center Is the New Edge." One of the things we've been seeing is that the edge has gotten incredibly predictable—I don't think it's very fresh anymore, because it's so focused on itself.' " [3]

As big of a relief as it is to hear a trend forecaster suggest that the whole concept of hip has played itself out, that the Man has succeeded in squeezing all the blood there is out of the turnip of Cool, we've still got to shake free of Cool's chilly and claustrophobic dominion, and take a step forward into the light. We must seize our chance of escaping slavery to the corpocratic-political-socio-fascist conformity machine (which I will continue to call "the Man", in deference to the Summer of Love—a hopeful time, despite how things have turned out so far.)

Dorkismo is for the free, nay, the hell-bent pursuit of happiness for everyone, for each in his own way, against spineless conformity and empty materialism. As we will see, nothing less than the great creative destiny of Western Civ. hangs in the balance.

Dorkismo. Know it. Live it. Let's begin.

May the Dorks Be With You

Daphne started asking questions, and I began answering them, because I know all the answers. But to answer the questions means I have to wear my Star Wars *visor, and so I put it on, because I am a nerd, and Daphne was stunned at the lengths of my nerdity. The look on her face was priceless when she realized, once and for all, that I was the biggest dork she had ever known, and that I was not embarrassed to admit that I owned a fake lightsaber (in public) or that I still wear* Star Wars *shirts, and that I am start-ing to get so excited about the third movie even though I know everybody good dies except Obi-Wan and Yoda, and that I broke down and bought the pregnant Padme action figure, because I could not resist the lure of a 3 3/4" action figure that was pregnant with Luke Skywalker and Princess Leia.*

http://www.lissapynn.com/blog/ (a good blog!)

(One.)

If you're too young (or old) to remember, you can scarcely conceive of the excitement that *Star Wars* generated from the moment it came out in 1977. Lines stretched around theatres all over the world, with people waiting three and four hours just to see it. There were no Internets or cell phones then— there wasn't even a VCR at home, not quite yet—and hordes of "kids of all ages" watched *Star Wars* over and over again, all summer long.

But even in those days, admitting that you loved *Star Wars* could get you a bad rap, as in, you must be really childish and naive if you openly enjoyed a kids' movie where the good guys win. You had to be a dork to love it, and did we ever. The dorks in their millions joined to embrace this playful, imaginative and entertaining story. *Star Wars* and the world it created immediately became a dork refuge: a haven of safety and freedom for the unabashed; a permanent, endless sanctuary, as it turned out.

Quite a lot of the highbrows were blown away by the Force right from the beginning, including the venerable J.G. Ballard, who wrote, "It is engaging, brilliantly designed, acted with real charm, full of verve and visual ingenuity,"[4] though he managed to hedge his bets a moment later: "It's also totally unoriginal, feebly plotted, instantly forgettable and an acoustic nightmare." Maybe so, but on its release, *Star Wars* also took in over $100 million in three months' time—not forgetting that movies didn't enjoy the huge releases they do today, or that ticket prices then averaged less than $2.50. The first installment of *Star Wars* alone has taken in over three-quarters of a billion dollars, so far.

There were two reasons for the paradigm-shattering success of *Star Wars*: one was the sensual wallop of the movie, with its spectacular, theatrical music and its bleeding-edge special effects ("lightspeed" in particular, where the stars lengthen and then shoot you like a bullet through space and time;) the other was the nakedly emotional appeal of a story in which the hero and his friends defeat an extra-villainous villain against impossible odds.

A good and well-known case can be made that this is exactly what we need most from movies and even from fiction in general: an escape from the cares of daily life, a fairytale in which everything comes right in the end; if not for ourselves, then for some imagined character whose triumphs we can experience vicariously. Far from being simple-minded or primitive, that may be the most vital function of storytelling, nothing less than a human imperative (for more on this point, see John Gardner's *On Moral Fiction* and E.M. Forster's *Aspects of the Novel.*) For George Lucas to respond to that imperative as seriously as he did was the dorkismo-packed move of the late 20th century. He would spend the next thirty years being pilloried for it, and lavished with wealth beyond the dreams of avarice for it. For the same thing! He was basically pelted with gold bricks from that moment forward. Lucas became the greatest populist in film history, a *billionaire* who is rarely mentioned in speaking of the great directors of the 1970s. He described the genesis of *Star Wars* this way:

> When I did *[American] Graffiti,* I discovered that
> making a positive film is exhilarating. I thought,
> Maybe I should make a film like this for even
> younger kids. *Graffiti* was for sixteen-year-olds; this
> *[Star Wars]* is for ten-and twelve-year-olds, who have
> lost something even more significant than the

teenager. I saw that kids today don't have any fantasy life the way we had—they don't have Westerns, they don't have pirate movies ...[5]

So many adults love *Star Wars* that people seem to forget that it was made explicitly as a kids' movie—hence the curiously sexless hero and heroine, the stagy swordplay, the unlikely, Arthurian hero, plucked from obscurity to fulfill a high destiny, and the absolute triumph of Good over Evil. These were powerful conventions that Lucas had himself been thrilled by—even redeemed by—as a kid (he had grown up a lonely outcast, especially susceptible to stories of unlikely heroes.) *Star Wars* has a curiously nostalgic feel, pleasantly at odds with the glossy, gorgeously futuristic world in which the story takes place (not accidentally, "a long, long time ago.")

Then as now, "entertainment" and "art" were widely seen as mutually exclusive. Lucas's famous colleagues—Coppola,

flickr photo by M@rcello), from the collection "Guerre Stellari," creative commons

Scorsese, Polanski, Altman, Friedkin, Ashby—had spent the previous ten years rebelling against the *Sound of Music* feel-good approach to storytelling, using instead the disillusionment created by Vietnam and Nixon's downfall to fuel a dark appetite for cynical, nihilistic stories like *The Godfather, Five Easy Pieces, M*A*S*H* and *Taxi Driver,* all of which were considered Art with a capital A by the people who made them, every one of whom had unending contempt for "popcorn pictures." Though many of these movies (*films!*—sorry) really are thought-provoking, beautiful and truthful—made with such enormous skill and creativity that they've held up perfectly, their appeal intact decades later—others have come to seem pointlessly bleak, didactic and self-indulgent; the dank, seedy bottom of the Me Generation barrel. With *Star Wars*, George Lucas did much to restore the traditional values of pure entertainment, the values he'd himself received from the movies, back to the movies.

The conventional wisdom is that by 1977, America was ready to be dumbed down by the corpocrats, and sold a heap of action figures with their Happy Meals. The trouble with this theory is that George Lucas was a super dork, but he was very far from being a yahoo. A *wunderkind* of the USC film school who won every student prize going, he was one of Francis Ford Coppola's earliest and closest associates; they met in 1967, when Lucas was twenty-three, and the slightly older Coppola became his mentor. Lucas was an intellectual, an experimental filmmaker from the start. Eventually he would set out to make popular entertainment, but he began in the avant-garde; they were his personal Establishment, and his relationship with them was always both intimate and tenuous. How he suffered, like the great big dork he was! He didn't even like cocaine or sleeping around. In the crowd Lucas ran with, that was about as subversive as you could get.

Even his wife Marcia openly regretted Lucas's success—she had abandoned editing *Star Wars* to work on the far groovier *New York, New York* with Martin Scorsese—saying: "There are so few good films, and part of me thinks *Star Wars* is partly responsible for the direction the industry has gone in, and I feel badly about that." She was not alone in this assessment. William Friedkin said: "*Star Wars* swept all the chips off the table. What happened with *Star Wars* was like when McDonald's got a foothold, the taste for good food just disappeared." Paul Schrader said: "*Star Wars* was the film that ate the heart and the soul of Hollywood."

In reality, the conventional narrative structure of "victory snatched from the jaws of defeat" had been held in abeyance during the era of Coppola, Schrader and Scorsese, but movie audiences had been longing for it. The dam had already broken the year before *Star Wars*, when *Rocky* bizarrely won the Best Picture Oscar over *All the President's Men, Bound for Glory, Network,* and *Taxi Driver.* That was early 1976, the Bicentennial Year, and American optimism was rising like the phoenix. A cynic might also observe that the stage was being set for the cowboy Ronald Reagan to come riding in, six-guns at the ready.

In this environment, Lucas was both a rebel against the art crowd and a populist hero. "Authority" to Lucas had been represented by Francis Ford Coppola, his former partner and mentor, and by all their superior, intellectual, anti-populist generation. "My life is kind of a reaction against Francis's life," Lucas has said. "I'm his antithesis."

⟡

(Two.)

Don Coppola

In 1970, Coppola very nearly followed the lead of every director in town by refusing to direct *The Godfather*. In a weird demonstration of me-too conformity posing as counterculturalism, Coppola said: "I was into the New Wave and Fellini and, like all the kids of my age, we wanted to make those kinds of films. So the book represented the whole kind of idea I was trying to avoid in my life." Bob Evans, the producer, had decided that he was going to need an Italian to direct *The Godfather* in order to be able to "smell the spaghetti," and Coppola, then a relative nobody, needed a job. Had he not been deep in debt, Coppola would never even have considered doing a "commercial movie." He asked his partner at American Zoetrope, George Lucas, "Should I do this?"

"I don't see any choice here, Francis," the ever-practical Lucas replied. [6]

In the event, the raging success of *The Godfather* went straight to the director's oversized head. He bought an airplane, a helicopter, houses, jukeboxes, a Mercedes limousine, a radio station. He was a runaway train who would end by burning through $30 million in 1970s dollars on *Apocalypse Now* (originally budgeted at $12 million,) and then crushing his own studio under the fiasco of *One from the Heart* (or *One Through the Heart,* as Hollywood wags took to calling it.) Coppola went bankrupt in 1982. His was not the only trainwreck in town; Friedkin, Cimino, Schrader, Towne, Rafelson, Ashby, and many others were smashed up right alongside him. A preponderance of the New Hollywood bad boys collapsed, the victims of drugs, hubris and just general brake failure, never to rise to their former heights again (the exception to this being Scorsese, who came back from his own 80s debacle to rise to—and remain at—the top of his profession.)

A convergence of factors helped to propel George Lucas forward—the loss of purpose suffered by the burned-out Me Generation, the slow but inexorable coalescing of profit-driven corporate power in the media, the shocking realization that dragon-heaps of money could be minted by putting movie-themed toys in Happy Meals—and the fact that by 1976, America was getting tired of nihilism and ready to feel good again, to be entertained. Much of this tended to obscure the fact that *Star Wars* didn't just rush in to fill the commercial vacuum left by the 70s flameouts; it was a deliberate, thoughtful attempt to restore something missing in American culture.

The script for *Star Wars*, two and a half years in the writing, was a scholarly enterprise based on Lucas's close, careful reading of Joseph Campbell, Castaneda and a ton of other books on the subject of myth and folkore. As he explained to Campbell's biographers:

> I came to the conclusion after *American Graffiti* that what's valuable for me is to set standards, not to show people the world the way it is...around the period of this realization...it came to me that there really was no modern use of mythology... The Western was possibly the last generically American fairy tale, telling us about our values. And once the Western disappeared,

Rita Molnár

nothing has ever taken its place. In literature we were going off into science fiction ... so that's when I started doing more strenuous research on fairy tales, folklore, and mythology, and I started reading Joe's books. Before that I hadn't read any of Joe's books...It was very eerie because in reading *The Hero with a Thousand Faces* I began to realize that my first draft of *Star Wars* was following classic motifs...so I modified my next draft according to what I'd been learning about classical motifs and made it a little bit more consistent.[7]

Lucas may never have had much of a groove quotient, but these authentically contrarian ideas pierced to the very heart of the Zeitgeist. *American Graffiti* had already established him as a nostalgist and a crowd-pleaser. He drew on the deep reservoir of his own escapist childhood passions and gave them back to the public. Audiences loved his work, not because it was foolish or because they were dumb, but because it was fresh and legitimate in every way, absolutely true to the basic contract between artist and audience. *Rocky* was a relatively solipsistic, egotistical and simple-minded story that satisfied many of the same urges, but the far more subtle *Star Wars* touched on themes of personal responsibility and political conscience, loyalty, talent and friendship, all wrapped in a rock-ribbed anti-authoritarian message that drew in millions of young minds by asking them to test their own convictions. For all its faults, *Star Wars* delivered completely, unselfishly, innocently, and without the arrogance or imitativeness that crippled so many of Lucas's colleagues. "I consciously set about to re-create myths and the classic mythological motifs," Lucas said. Did Friedkin, Schrader and their contemporaries, that gang of brilliant but coke-addled narcissists whose careers collapsed under the weight of their own megalomania, seriously believe that they had anything more valuable to offer the public than this? In a 2001 census, when asked what their religion was, 390,000 Britons wrote in "Jedi."[8] Did William Friedkin invent a religion? No! Not even a dorky, half-joking anti-religion.

It has been noted that the story of Luke Skywalker and Darth Vader mirrors the relationship of Lucas and Coppola very neatly. Both are skilled warriors who serve the Force, but one has gone bad; Coppola/Vader appeals to Lucas/Skywalker to join the dark side, where his power will increase, where they can take over the universe—but Skywalker refuses, despite the revelation that he is, in fact, the son of his foe. George Lucas's every move was a bid for more and more independence—from Coppola, from the studios, from anything that would interfere with his personal and artistic freedom.

In closing, the perceptive observer will concede that *Star Wars* is no less subtle a document than *Taxi Driver.* Here are two very specific visions of the world, conceived for the purposes of entertainment and reflection. A lot can be learned by studying the public response to both. And we could go still further than

Lucas, I am your father.

this. Do we want to live in the world of Luke Skywalker, or the world of Travis Bickle? For the dorks of the late 1970s, there was no contest—nor, for that matter, is there any contest for the dorks of the 21st century:

> Okay, so if I saw Natalie walking toward me...I think I'd be like holy shit what should I do. I would probably WANT to talk and talk about star wars and cold mountain but I don't think she'd take the time to talk to a random gal off the street like that, haha I don't know. I probably wouldn't be able to think up something nice and witty soon enough and then she'd pass me and I'd probably just smile and say hi. Most likely, if no one else was bothering her. OR

> I'd go totally crazy just right there and be like 'PADME AMIDALA!!!' and show her my jedi moves or something and she'd think I was the biggest dork. haha.
>   - Lyra , www.natalieportman.com[9]

Heaven is other people

There's a beautiful, snotty blonde girl seated at the counter of a diner. Nearby, an oddly pleasant-looking tousled guy, his face smeared with mustard and ketchup, is fast losing his battle with a massive sandwich. Suddenly, the sandwich's innards escape *en masse* into his soup bowl, and, flailing, he overturns his iced tea onto the counter. Now the blonde girl is pointing her new Sprint PCS Camera Phone in his direction. Does this prize dork even realize that he is having his picture taken? Either way, he gives her a friendly, ketchup-covered thumbs-up as she snaps his photo, her face full of malice and dark mirth.

"Gina check this out. I'm sitting next to your new *boyfriend.*"

Gina is a lovely, serious-looking brunette seated on the hood of a car beside the well-known Sprint spokesman in his black overcoat and tie. The two of them examine the smiling, ketchupy image of Sandwich Guy that has just appeared on Gina's fancy new phone, as the blonde's voice wafts over the speaker:

Screenshots and voice clips simulated

"Don't you just *love* your new boyfriend?"

Gina turns to the Sprint guy and says gravely, "I *do* love him."

"As long as you're happy," he replies.

Hardly anybody had even seen such a novel and interesting contraption as a Sprint PCS Camera Phone in those long-ago days of 2003. But in the Internet brouhaha that followed, nobody talked about the putative subject of the commercial (how the new camera phones might affect social interaction); instead, Sprint's tiny tale of the ineffability of love split the nation into two irreconcilable camps, staring at one another in mute incomprehension across a yawning chasm. There were those who adored the commercial, and those who loathed it, and there was nobody in between. How could a 30-second commercial create such a gash in the fabric of American society? Well, if you believed in the possibility of loving a total dork, you were surprised and delighted by the commercial, not least because such stuff is never shown on television, while those who have their doubts on that score were made confused or unhappy by it, or even supposed themselves to have been played.

It takes a super dork to capture the true essence of Sprint's masterwork, and here he is:[10]

> Joined: 03 Jan 2002
> Posts: 293
> Location: Irvine, CA
> Posted: Thu Oct 30, 2003 3:50 pm
>
> This is my favorite commercial:
> "Here's our jingle for Goldfish

We wrote a song for Goldfish

The wholesome snack that smiles back
until you bite their heads off!
See the fishes swimming...
Oh look the pretzel's winning...

Didn't that make you feel good about Goldfish?

Here's our Jingle for Goldfish
Crunchy little Goldfish
Oh good we're at the part
Where we show that they're baked and not fried

Did you know they're made with real cheese
Even though they look like fishies

The snack that smiles back: Goldfish."

I CANNOT GET ENOUGH of the "Oh look the
pretzel's winning" part. I get this good feeling when-
ever I hear it (just like the next line of the song asks
me about!), and I always try to sing along. I feel that
I could watch it a million times.

I also adore the one for Sprint mobile phones
where a girl is in a diner next to the clumsiest man
in the world who, while attempting to eat an incredibly messy sandwich, smears ketchup and mustard
all over his face, squirts lemon juice in his eye, and
knocks over his glass of soda in the process.

The girl snaps a photo of him (in a completely

unrespectable state, giving a big old corny thumbs up) with her mobile phone/camera and sends it to her best friend? sister? with the message, "Hey, check this out. I'm sitting next to your new boyfriend. Don't you just love your new boyfriend?"

Her friend, who is sitting with the Sprint problem-solver-guy, receives the photo and message, turns to the Sprint guy and in the most sincere, unusual way, says, "I do love him".

"As long as you're happy," he replies.

GAH! It's just so NICE!! Do you not love this commercial??!

And here I am, using T-Mobile like a sucker.

Many weighed in on the side of GAH! Man, including Television without Pity, who wrote:

> I hated it the first time I saw it, because I thought that girl was a bitch for picking on this dorky guy just for being a dorky guy, and I was so irritated by the "we are superior and must laugh at the dorky guy" tone, but then the end totally redeems the whole thing. And when I described it to Johanna, and how at the end Gina says, "I do love him," she said "Aww," and I love him too, by the way. And the way she says "I do love him" makes me happy every single time. I want a whole series of ads about Gina and the dorky guy getting together, and also an ad where the bitchy girl gets her comeuppance for being such a snot.

(Gah! Me too. Didn't happen, sadly.)

There was even a dorkily Catholic interpretation of the commercial on "Trust the Truth, A Catholic Blog by Matthew G. Collins":[11]

> **God's Love, Brought to You by the Sprint Man**
> My favorite commercial is one for Sprint in which a nerdy, socially inept young man is eating a very large and unwieldy sandwich at a lunch counter, making an incredible mess of it in the spirit of Red Skelton. […]
>
> Isn't that how God is with each of us? No matter how goofy or unworthy the world may think we are, no matter how stupid or unworthy we really are, God loves us. He sees through all the externals into the nobleness of our heart. He loves us more than our own mother loves us.
>
> That's the way the Lord is with us!

Yes, all this was very nice. But …

Across the divide was ranged a gang of desperate souls who disagreed with those sunny characters; who saw all sorts of weird and even sinister messages lurking in a cellphone commercial.

> Nov 12, 2003, 10:51 pm
>
> I hate the new Sprint Wireless Picture Phones, or whatever they are. My wife has one, but that was before we saw the ad campaign, which is based on being cruel to the hopeless, the downtrodden souls

that even God has turned His back to. There's one where a 'hot' girl is sitting in a diner, and this poor, probably mentally challenged fool is trying to eat a sandwich. He's making a mess of it and himself, and the 'hot' girl, while secretly pointing her camera phone at him, waves. He smiles a horrible but friendly smile back, and she sends the pic to her friend. "This is your new boyfriend. Don't you just love your new boyfriend" She receives the picture and deadpans "I do love him" to some well-suited jackass sitting next to her. He says, "As long as you're happy."

SPRINT has gotten around to venomously mocking mentally inferior people with their ads. Not just stupid, like the 3 Stooges, but actually, literally RETARDED people. If you are so fortunate to have more than a double digit IQ and good looks, like the 'hot' chick with the camera, exactly how beautiful is it to turn your bile on those who clearly cannot defend themselves? This poor fellow wasn't blessed with good looks or brains, and without those, sophistication is going to be difficult to acchieve, but it's people like these who have the purest hearts. I hate Sprint for trying to have an easy laugh with us at his expense. Have some balls. Go after powerful, shallow, or stuffy people. Evil.

This guy was rocketed back into a hellish cauldron of adolescent insecurity and pain by the sight of a snotty blonde girl taking advantage of Sandwich Guy's innocence and trust.

Nobody could love such an obviously flawed being as Sandwich Guy, he thinks! The end of the commercial must be a booby trap, then, like those snares laid by the 'cool' kids in order to dupe the unwary, and Gina was just another cruelly beautiful, deceitful fraud, a 21st-century Estella, a false-hearted liar. Soon, a response came:

> I hope the guy who wrote that ad gets pinned between two colliding cars and then sodomized by a bull.
>
> Thot I was the only one who caught that underlying msg. You are spot on with your judgment of Sprint's ads.

How amazingly furious these two are! They were gabbing on a comics blog.[12] Two guys on a comics blog who do not understand the possibility that we might be able to love a guy who is covered in condiments! The really alarming thing about this is that they were on a comics blog, which (maybe foolishly) makes me suppose that they are liable to be pretty dorked-out themselves, and so, do they really think that everybody including God has "turned His back to", or on, rather, them?! But it's not true, comix dudes, we *do* love you, and so does God, according to Matthew G. Collins.

In reality, this blonde cellphone-photo chick is just another common or garden Mean Girl who wants to embarrass all the dorks into ditching their idiosyncrasies and becoming "normal," like she is (though less "cool.") As if! Could it be that some dorkishly-inclined persons (like the comix dudes—?) have been forced into an uneasy compromise with their enemies, figured out how to "pass", and they are shamefully hiding their true dork nature, or revealing it only in secret? Maybe, and maybe that is a really sad thing. If they can get some dorkismo, they need no longer fear any blonde cell-phone-photo villainesses. Sandwich Guy is just such a hero, fearlessly brimming with dorkismo, a guiding light to us all. No wonder Gina loves him.

Only the most hardened cynic would straight up refuse to believe that a beautiful girl could love a sloppy but sincere guy. Faces are washable! Which would remove ketchup, but not sincerity or kindness. The redemptive capacity of love comprehends the real face beneath the ketchup. Thank goodness, then, for Rippin' Barslut, who had no trouble rippin' straight to the heart of the matter, on the ClubPlanet message boards.

> Rippin' Barslut
> Join Date: Sep 1999
> Location: a tiny mushroom outside your home
> Posts: 14,089
> That blonde in the commercial is a mean bitch for doing that :-0
> but his girls' reaction proves the power of love :)

Thus and thus the contrast between those possessed of dorkismo and those without was displayed in the starkest terms: Gina loves Sandwich Guy, v. she loves him not. One couldn't help feeling that there must be a definitive answer to this question. So which was it? Within a matter of weeks, the answer had been reported in the *Chicago Tribune.*

Tribune columnist Eric Zorn had weighed in with some stunningly obtuse remarks re: the commercial in the context of an article about camera phones and privacy. Apparently he'd had a conversation with one Ron Nunes, a deranged District Commissioner in Elk Grove Park, Illinois, who was serving his community by attempting to have cell phone cameras literally banned "in locker areas, shower facilities and restrooms at park facilities":

> [Nunes] said his inspiration came [...] when he saw that extremely icky "new boyfriend?" TV spot.
>
> In that commercial, a young woman sees her friend's new boyfriend sloppily scarfing down a sandwich at a lunchroom counter. She produces her Sprint PCS camera-equipped cell phone, snaps a photo of the young man in flagrante disgusto, and transmits it to her friend along with the catty question, "Don't you just love your new boyfriend?"
>
> "It's a big reminder of all the potential problems," said Nunes of the commercial.
>
> "Taking pictures of people surreptitiously is not considered good form, and we don't condone it," said Dan Wilinsky, director of media relations for Sprint PCS. "You'll notice that the guy with the mess on his face is giving a thumbs-up for the camera. That's an expression of tacit approval."
>
> But Nunes and I, at least, see it as clumsy flirtation by a numbskull who has no idea that what looks like a telephone in the young woman's hand is actually a digital camera. And it underscores that— no matter what the manufacturers intend—these hybrid devices can be spy gadgets.[13]

Fortunately, Eric Zorn's readership was not about to let him get away with any of that bushwah. Complaints rolled in, and to give him all the credit in the world, it took just three days for him to end the mystery forever:

> "It's 50-50, from what I hear," said Mark Sweeney, 38, the creative director at the Publicis & Hal Riney ad agency who created the spot for Sprint PCS. "I was trying to leave it a little ambiguous at the end, but I've been surprised by all the conversations and arguments about it."
>
> "The two girls are best friends," he said, going into the backstory. "The guy is just some guy at the lunch counter. They've never met him."
>
> But, Sweeney said, the blond woman's attempt to make a joke at his expense backfires because Gina— the name is a tribute to Sweeney's wife— [(!)] loves Slob Guy at first sight.
>
> "She loves how un-self-conscious he is," he said. "She loves how he gives the thumbs up to the camera even though he's a mess. She loves him for him."[14]

That's the way dorkismo is with us!

björn türoque

the world's
second-best
air guitarist rawks
an
adoring public

Are YOU into BJÖRN?

*Björn, you very nearly won the national title at the Key Club here in L.A. last month.
To what do you attribute the victory of your rival, Fatima "The Rockness Monster" Hoang?*

The Rockness had several things going for him. Primarily, he had Asian Fury. It's
the third time he's beaten me. This term was coined by C. Diddy, the 2000 U.S.
Air Guitar champion, who used it--aptly--to describe himself. Little did I know
I would be facing the same titanic force for years to come.

Dear Björn, what is under your bed?

Three naked 18-year-old girls.

Björn, can you comment on the idea of air guitar as art?

I think that an artist is someone that inspires others to become artists.
In that way, air guitar is the ultimate art form.

*I understand that you sometimes interview yourself. What's the difference between
Dan Crane and Björn Turoque?*

Björn is a rock star, with all the trappings. I'm a cocky, sex-crazed, drug-taking,
vomiting-all-over-my-Versace-jacket-that-my-fans-bought-for-me rock star.
Dan Crane is obviously an intellectual, primarily concerned with the higher
pursuits. Our common ground is music, and its power to rock.

*Björn, do you watch The Dating Game? I would love if you were on there,
and you would choose me! Would you ever go on The Dating Game?*

Um, Björn doesn't really need to go on the dating game. Björn has many
air groupies at his disposal. If you wanted to play a mock dating game with two
of your hawt friends, though, that's cool.

Björn, I love hamburgers! I was wondering what are your favorite foods?

I like sushi, and I like basically anything raw and wet.

Dear Björn, when you take a shower, do you dry your hair first or your feet first?

I don't dry my feet, it's best not to touch one's feet. I only let young girls
touch my feet.

Do you ever get whipped or scolded at all, Björn? You seem so sweet.

I am a glutton for punishment, and I like to misbehave, and then be
reined in, so to speak.

I'm kind of embarrassed to ask, but what kind of girls do you like?

Young girls. I like basically any girl that's up for a rawkin' good time who likes
loud music, smoky bars, good food and wants to cuddle up with a good book.

Ťřəin Men

Happiness is not obtained through self-gratification, but through fidelity to a worthy purpose.

HELEN KELLER

The foreign words most closely approximating the American "dork" are the British *anorak,* and *otaku,* which is Japanese. The former was originally associated with trainspotting[15] and pirate radio fans (an anorak being a kind of heavy raincoat such as one might wear whilst waiting around for trains, or visiting Radio Caroline in the Irish Sea) and the latter, with anime.

"Otaku" is actually an honorific form of address, like *vous* or *usted;* literally, "your honorable dwelling-place." (In Japanese, "o" in front of a word means something like "honorable," which is why "ocha" is the polite way of saying "tea." Actually it is pretty much the only way of saying "tea," unless you are an entirely disreputable character, like a bandit in a movie.) So the primary meaning of *otaku* is just a more formal, classical way of saying *anata* or "you."

Several possibilities have been mooted as the source of the contemporary idiomatic meaning of *otaku*, the most credible coming from anime producer and lecturer Toshio Okada; according to him, the creators of the 1982 *Super Dimension Fortress Macross,* Shoji Kawamori and Haruhiko Mikimoto, affected this refined form of address when they were students together at Keio University (a very fancy school, whose graduates include Japanese notables from Junichiro Koizumi to Yohji Yamamoto.) Kawamori and Mikimoto gave their characters in the *Macross* series the same turn of phrase, and it spread from there via fans of the hugely popular *Macross* as a token of involvement in anime culture, much the same way that an American might say, "live long and prosper" as a friendly indication of dorkismo (or, at least, Star Trekkismo.)[16]

In this dork incarnation, *otaku* has various shades of meaning—most commonly, it's still used to describe the aficionado of anime or video games whose obsessive interests have rendered him socially inept. The *otaku* capital of Japan is Akihabara Electric Town, a shopping district in Tokyo teeming with neon, robots and video arcades. And dorks. William Gibson described *otaku* in the 1996 novel *Idoru:*

> "Masahiko is seventeen," Mitsuko said. "He is a
> 'pathological-techno-fetishist-with-social-deficit,'"
> this last all strung together like one word, indicating
> a concept that taxed the lexicon of the ear-clips.
> Chia wondered briefly if it would be worth running
> it through her Sandbenders, whose translation func-
> tions updated automatically whenever she ported.
> "A what?"
> "Otaku," Mitsuko said carefully in Japanese. The
> translation burped its clumsy word string again.

In Japan, you can be an *otaku* about any number of things—you might be a cooking *otaku*, or a pasokon *otaku* (into personal computers) or a gunji *otaku* (into militaria.) The common feature is that the intensity of involvement is linked to "social-deficit." In this way, *otaku* is a lot like our *nerd* and *dork;* we also have computer nerds and vinyl nerds and model train dorks, as the Japanese do. But social skill is super-highly valued in Japan—one is expected to step up to the plate and not just perform but excel socially, whether in school, fashion, work, sports, or elegant manners and conversation in general—so traditionally, there has not been much truck with social ineptitude over there. For a long time *otaku* was basically a slur, and people would almost never refer to themselves this way. Matters were made far worse by the fact that in the 1980s, a serial murderer of young girls was dubbed the "*Otaku* Killer" by the Japanese tabloid press because of his immense collection of nearly 6,000 movies, among them pornographic anime. The nickname turned out to be a total stretch, because it eventually emerged that the *Otaku* Killer had very little anime in his collection, wasn't particularly interested in it; also, at least one of the murders mimicked a notorious series of fake snuff movies called *The Guinea Pig Films,* which were not *otaku* material at all. But the idea of the socially-withdrawn anime collector/violent criminal fired the public imagination, whether such a person existed or not, and *otaku* became a dirtier word than ever.

In his book *Wrong About Japan,* the Australian novelist Peter Carey describes his own fascination with this concept at length, observing, "The more you try to pin down *otaku*, the more wriggly it gets." Anime author and scholar (and self-described *otaku*) Yuka Minakawa tried and tried to explain it to him: "It's not respectful, it's discriminatory. It's like calling you 'sir' when I don't really mean it. It's ironic, sarcastic." She then made Carey a drawing of "a fat teenager with a schlumpy T-shirt and a bad complexion": "*Otaku*," she said, pushing it across the table. "[...] among the *otaku* community there are many of us who will laugh and make fun of this sort of person. We used to have a badge, like the *Ghostbusters* badge,

The cover to the Macross Memorial *DVD Box Set*

with a red line drawn across this type of figure."

The Japanese were already mistrustful enough of techno-fetishist-social-deficit *otaku* by the early 1990s, when *hikikomori* began to be discussed in earnest. The victims of *hikikomori*, an acute form of social withdrawal, are generally young men who shut themselves up in their rooms, venturing out only for the occasional family meal. Sufferers might not leave their parents' houses for years at a stretch, and they have no friends or social contacts at all. *Hikikomori* is said to begin quite often as *tokokyohi* (school phobia); some believe that the intense pressure in Japanese schools and the poor career prospects for indifferent students are responsible for both afflictions. But when the *New York Times* ran a story about them in January of 2006, the behavior of *hikikomori* sounded not only a lot like *otaku*-derived "social-deficit" taken to the last extreme, but also uncannily like the American extremes of nerd behavior—what we've seen, for example, in movies like *Fast, Cheap and Out of Control, Ghost World* and *The 40-Year-Old Virgin*.[17] It's obvious enough that there are misfits in every country who have lost all faith in the possibility that there is a place in the world for them. In any case, the uncomfortable association between *otaku* and *hikikomori* didn't help the social prospects for *otaku* at all. And then suddenly, something amazing happened.

Maybe people began to realize that there might be more to *otaku* (at least in the sense of "passionate obsessive," in William Gibson's phrase) than just social ineptitude; maybe there was a backlash against the unjust connection that had been made between *otaku* and criminals. Whatever the cause, by 2005 Japan was ready to embrace the fantastic tale (by way of the book, four manga adaptations, a movie, a play and a TV series) of *Densha Otoko* ("Train Man.") Based on real events that took place in 2004 (though no one has yet been identified as the real Densha,) *Densha Otoko* is the story of a typical Akihabara *otaku* (called Yamada in the amazing TV series)[18] who one day rescues a beautiful girl from the unwelcome attentions of a drunken brawler on a train. Never having taken such a risk in his life before, Yamada is astonished at the warmth of the thanks he receives from the girl, and from the other female passengers on the train. Before they part ways, the women make sure to get Yamada's address, so that they can thank him again for his bravery. He then dashes home to post anonymously about the exciting episode on a 2channel[19] internet chat for lonely single guys.

Understand that until now, he has been too shy even to post on an internet chat for lonely single guys. He begins, "I'm mostly a lurker …"

Now the action begins, as the chat residents begin to grow interested in the story of the "Train Man." A thank-you gift arrives from the beautiful girl, exactly as one poster has predicted! Two delicate teacups. Now what? Everyone has an opinion … and when it is discovered that the cups come from the French luxury label Hermès, all hell breaks loose and advice rains down in torrents on our hero regarding the proper etiquette for gifts and phone calls and eventually, as matters progress, on haircuts, clothes and restaurants. They nickname the girl "Hermès" and indulge themselves in every kind of wild conjecture as they wait for Densha's next report; they write steamy imaginary dialogue for the couple, and

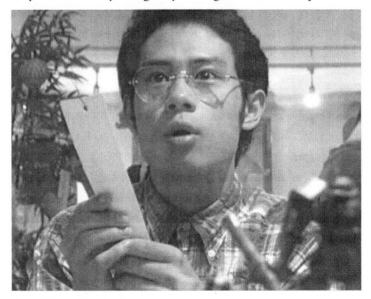

Atsushi Ito as Densha Otoko

Manga adaptation of Train Man, *English Version*

stampede to a fancy Tokyo boutique to buy the kind of tea Hermès likes best (actual sales of 'Benoist' tea are said to have tripled as a result.) Panic, excitement, fear and hope burst out among the 2channellers with every obsessively-dissected detail of the burgeoning romance; by the time the story nears its breathtaking climax, some two months after the incident on the train, half Japan seems to have been brought to the brink of nervous collapse over the question of how and when (or even whether) the Train Man will confess his love. Anonymous posters on the thread describe their own newfound courage, gained from witnessing the extraordinary transformation of Densha, the former *otaku* who manages, bit by bit, to conquer his shyness and gaucherie in pursuit of the gentle and beautiful Hermès.

Some of the original 2channel thread has been translated into English online; there's no other way to say this, the innocent and pure heart of Densha shines even through the translated Internet chat transcript. He is just such a good guy. It's very difficult to imagine how the original transcript could have been even partially faked (that is, faked à la James Frey,) since it's in a public chat archive, but whether genuine or "staged," it's easy to see how this story of a worthy young person coming out of his shell to find love became so insanely popular. Added to this was the novelty of experiencing it all along with Train Man's 2channel friends; their fanatical involvement in Densha's adventures gives an entirely new kind of piquancy to the unusual, slowly blossoming love story.

The redemption of *otaku* in *Densha Otoko* is a promising sign for fans of dorkismo. When you consider that the Japanese—that ancient and cultivated people, who nevertheless have been much derided for their snobbery, conformity and groupthink—showed themselves so willing to help and champion Train Man, the world's biggest pathological-techno-fetishist-with-social-deficit, it is so touching, so encouraging. That first the Japanese 2channel audience, and then the whole nation, went so far as to consider Densha as a worthy object of interest and love, illustrates our theory with perfect aesthetic and moral precision; in a just and good society there is room enough for everyone to be accepted, to find his true self, and to achieve happiness. In the unfolding phenomenon of *Densha Otoko,* it was the Japanese themselves who rose to the apotheosis of dorkismo, who liberated themselves from their societal constraints and gave their allegiance to the higher wisdom.

Great Moments in Dorkismo, Vol. 1

Roger Ebert is a Great Big Dork

Every month or so, I get an anguished letter from a reader wanting to know how I could possibly have been so ignorant as to award three stars to, say, "Hidalgo" while dismissing, say, "Dogville" with two stars. This disparity between my approval of kitsch and my rejection of angst reveals me, of course, as a superficial moron who will do anything to suck up to my readers.

What these correspondents do not grasp is that to suck up to my demanding readers, I would do better to praise "Dogville." It takes more nerve to praise pop entertainment; it's easy and safe to deliver pious praise of turgid deep thinking. It's true, I loved "Anaconda" and did not think "The United States of Leland" worked, but does that mean I drool at the keyboard and prefer man-eating snakes to suburban despair?

Not at all. What it means is that the star rating system is relative, not absolute. When you ask a friend if "Hellboy" is any good, you're not asking if it's any good compared to "Mystic River," you're asking if it's any good compared to "The Punisher." And my answer would be, on a scale of one to four, if "Superman" (1978) is four, then "Hellboy" is three and "The Punisher" is two. In the same way, if "American Beauty" gets four stars, then "Leland" clocks in at about two.

Russ Myers and Roger Ebert
photo courtesy of Wikimedia Commons

And that is why "Shaolin Soccer," a goofy Hong Kong action comedy, gets three stars. It is piffle, yes, but superior piffle. If you are even considering going to see a movie where the players zoom 50 feet into the air and rotate freely in violation of everything Newton held sacred, then you do not want to know if I thought it was as good as "Lost in Translation."

Review of "Shaolin Soccer," collected in *Roger Ebert's Movie Yearbook 2005.*

Yay! is all.

et in Academia Ego

(One.)

In 1957, Norman Mailer wrote "The White Negro", a wacky essay about beatnik and jazz culture that prefigured the morphing of countercultural values into "hip consumerism," a term that describes how the Man, by appealing to your rebellious, radical, punk or hippie side, coerces you into buying things.

Despite commenting on Mailer's "astonishingly backwards racial views" and the way "his identification of black Americans with bodily pleasure, lack of inhibition, and sexual prowess conforms rather neatly to standard stereotypes and racial myths," Thomas Frank in *The Conquest of Cool* joined a boatload of modern sociologists in painting "The White Negro" as a triumph of the crystal ball: "This enormously important essay has never been adequately recognized for what must either

be counted its remarkable influence or its remarkable prognostication: Mailer here managed to predict the basic dialectic around which the cultural politics of the next thirty-five years would be structured."[20]

There's a lot more to the story of "The White Negro" than meets the eye. Mailer's vision of American culture emerged from a boiling cauldron of dissent and political upheaval; it was mixed-up, provisional and misguided from the start. In 1967 James Baldwin, who'd hung out with Mailer in Paris, wrote a splendid response to "The White Negro" called "The Black Boy looks at the White Boy." Though he characterized this essay as a "love letter" to Mailer, Baldwin did not scruple to make the main point:

> [...] the Negro jazz musicians, among whom we sometimes found ourselves, who really liked Norman, did not for an instant consider him as being even remotely "hip" and Norman did not know this and I could not tell him. He never broke through to them, at least not as far as I know; and they were far too "hip," if that is the word I want, even to consider breaking through to him. They thought he was a real sweet ofay cat, but a little frantic.[21]

What Baldwin failed to take into account was that Mailer didn't intend for any jazz musicians to consider him "hip;" what he really wanted was for the white intelligentsia in New York to consider him hip. Explaining the philosophy and argot of black jazz musicians in overheated English prose was

Mailer's ticket to the top of the ivory tower, and maybe the Time-Life Building, but nowhere else ... after all, Mailer didn't join a jazz combo in Paris any more than Susan Sontag quit the intellectual high life in order to put on drag shows. Mailer's intended audience didn't really care if his writing was incoherent; they were thrilled to hear a reactionary speaking, more or less, their own language; this was itself enough of a break in the monotony of *comme il faut* to suggest the possibility of real change in their own world. It was exciting to think about what it might be like to be a beatnik, and here was that Angry Young Man of Brooklyn via Paris to explain it to them. Sort of.

> One is Hip or one is Square (the alternative which each new generation coming into American life is beginning to feel), one is a rebel or one conforms, one is a frontiersman in the Wild West of American night life, or else a Square cell, trapped in the totalitarian tissues of American society, doomed willy-nilly to conform if one is to succeed.

Or:

> Knowing in the cells of his existence that life was war, nothing but war, the Negro (all exceptions admitted) could rarely afford the sophisticated inhibitions of civilization, and so he kept for his survival the art of the primitive, he lived in the enormous present, he subsisted for his Saturday night kicks, relinquishing the pleasures of his mind for the more

obligatory pleasures of the body, and in his music he gave voice to the character and quality of his existence, to his rage and the infinite variations of joy, lust, languor, growl, cramp, pinch, scream and despair of his orgasm. For jazz is orgasm, it is the music of orgasm, good orgasm and bad, and so it spoke across a nation, it had the communication of art even where it was watered, perverted, corrupted, and almost killed, it spoke in no matter what laundered popular way of instantaneous existential states to which some whites could respond, it was indeed a communication by art because it said, "I feel this, and now you do too."[22]

(Wowie!)

"The White Negro" wasn't cynical so much as luridly ambitious, and the writing itself is loopy and fun. Baldwin's "hip" friends were right; Mailer was a real sweet ofay cat, just a little frantic. Not "even remotely 'hip,'" however.

Weirdly, though, the very thing that Thomas Frank had found so prescient/influential was precisely the formal identification of "hipsters"

It was Aida Overton Walker's fault!

made by Mailer in "The White Negro." "… a figure Mailer called the hipster, an 'American existentialist' whose taste for jazz, sex, drugs, and the slang and mores of black society constituted the best means of resisting the encroachments of cold war and oppression."[23]

Frank goes on to argue that the "taste for jazz, sex, drugs," etc. eventually grew deep into the mainstream of society, so that it became necessary for the Man to co-opt and water down those values in order to sell everybody stuff, until those values had been well sapped of their original significance, of their political power, and of any real "rebellion" they'd ever possessed. Much as I admire Thomas Frank, though, we can begin by disabusing him of the notion that there was ever an iota of "rebellion" in Norman Mailer.

The essential flimsiness of Mailer's reactionary vision was evident to a number of observers quite early on. In "The White Negro and the Negro White" (1967), sociologist Gary T. Marx nailed the whole thing, articulating with terrific force the parallels between the white "hipster" reactionary mentality (unshaven, left politics, no job, high on pot—basically, "the opposite of what my parents and their friends are, in the guise of a political position,") and the black bourgeois reactionary mentality (more strict than strict, more clean than clean—in short, "the opposite of widespread assumptions about these lower-class black people with whom I can't stand being associated.")

> Negroes will show how middle-class they are and beats what white Negroes they are. What Negroes embrace wholeheartedly beats reject just as furiously.

The hipster behavior patterns which beats embrace and go out of their way to be identified with are the very behavior patterns that middle-class Negroes strongly reject. They have switched drummers and in so doing both may be hearing the beat not quite right, resulting in the misconception by Negroes of what it really means to be middle-class white and the misconception by beats of what it really means to be Negro.[24]

In other words White Negroes, well maybe, but with the emphasis on the "White." Mailer wasn't rebelling, he was *conforming*, albeit backhandedly, by claiming the position of brilliant insurrectionist, prodigal returned, interpreter of the forbidden, hidden counterculture, but living, working and publishing in the highest citadels of the educated white community.

The fact that Mailer was a fake rebel undercuts Frank's whole thesis; there was no authentic 'rebellion' in the first place, nothing to co-opt. We'll attend to the ramifications of that in a sec. But my more serious beef with Frank is this: in no way does he provide an accurate description of our relationship to consumerism, hip or otherwise. We most of us not only despise consumerism (or to cast a somewhat broader net, the whole of the Establishment,) we *understand* it all too well. Frank will agree with me that of the most popular writing, music and artworks of the last fifty years, an enormous proportion concerns itself with the sterility and shallowness of the Establishment: the Beatles, Don DeLillo, Terry Southern, William Gaddis, *The Sopranos, Mad Men,*

Damien Hirst, Jonathan Franzen, and shoot, if we're going to talk movies which one does not qualify, from *Network* to *Zoolander* to *Repo Man* to *American Beauty* to *Wall-E*. Frank's contention is that *American Beauty* is a consumer product; therefore, watch it and you've been co-opted by the Man. But surely, we can't seriously entertain the argument that the Beatles' anti-consumerist message was in any way lessened by the fact that it came on a piece of plastic that you had to buy in a shop? The message was bigger than the plastic, and we knew it. The plastic could never interfere with a message of that size and importance.

Aren't we smart enough to know exactly how and when we're being played? The truth is, we negotiate a certain amount of commerce with the Man *consciously;* just enough to get what we need and want out of the culture. It's flawed, we know how it's flawed, many of us are trying to address the flaws, but for the moment it's what we've got. Frank makes no attempt to understand the actual techniques by which "hip consumerism" is constantly resisted in real life. The Man is subtle and devious, yes, but we ourselves are equally so. Americans are by and large immune to and indeed contemptuous of all the Man's supposedly irresistible blandishments.

Take the many fans of Iggy Pop who heard the song "Lust for Life" weirdly used to flog Carnival Cruises, a perfect example of "hip consumerism." Did this mean that they went on a Carnival Cruise? Was the adman responsible reckoned all "rock and roll" for associating "Lust for Life" with going on a Carnival Cruise (though it goes without saying that the inconvenient phrase "with lickah an drugs" had to be snipped out?) Is it remotely possible that Iggy fans decided that

Carnival Cruises could not perhaps be quite so geriatric, if their adman likes Iggy Pop?—No! The answer to all these questions is No. I do hope that Mr. Osterberg laughed all the way to the bank, in his agreeably ravaged-sounding way. In the bigger scheme of things, it's a small recompense we're making him for *Raw Power.*

There is no "hip consumerism." There is only the attempt to persuade people to buy things, pitched in language and images we are supposed to find compelling. What we can say with authority is that nobody obeys the Man unquestioningly; we are keenly, painfully aware of the emptiness of consumer culture, no matter what attempts are made to co-opt this or that. The proof of that being that it's quite difficult and expensive even to try to persuade the public of anything, and that there are far more failures than successes among those who do try.

(Ťwø.)

What "The White Negro" really portended was "the dialectic around which" sociologists would come to ply their trade. To understand the real impact of "The White Negro," it is very helpful to consider Susan Sontag's equally influential (and possibly even crazier) "Notes on 'Camp' " (published seven years after "The White Negro," in *Partisan Review.*) Each is an ambitious, self-conscious intellectual's application essay for admission into the ranks of the "hip," in its latter-day sense of "countercultural elite." These flipped-out writings, deeply flawed and unintentionally hilarious as they are, however, also demonstrate how by the mid-century a primitive form of dorkismo was beginning to percolate throughout the literary world.

Though mass culture was a central concern of the philosophers and sociologists of the Frankfurt School starting in the 1930s, and for later theorists like Edward Shils and Herbert J. Gans, none of those writers personally ID'd with mass culture or counterculture in any way. Far from it. Shils actually said in 1959: "Some people dislike the working classes more than the middle classes, depending on their political backgrounds. But the real fact is that from an esthetic and moral standpoint, the objects of mass culture are repulsive to us."[25]

Where do I even begin with this, except to note that telling "us." Shils's pompous pronouncements speak for themselves. And it's not just Shils and his pal Gans, believe me. Before "The White Negro," cultural critics in general were invariably spectacularly condescending to both the consumers and producers of mass culture. After decades of professional sneering, the academy had effectively marooned itself on the intellectual high ground by the time the likes of Mailer and Sontag rolled up.

What makes "Notes on 'Camp' "" and "The White Negro" in retrospect so mind-blowing is the fact that their authors positively flaunted their personal familiarity and identification with the counterculture as itself a kind of intellectual or at least experiential chops—something that guys like Shils or Gans would never have done in a zillion years—and the resulting documentation of cultural fluency turned out to be irresistibly attractive and powerful, so much more powerful than anything the intelligentsia had managed to cough up in decades that it set in motion currents of ever-increasing force and conviction. The ideas and language of the counterculture presented in a highbrow setting retain a refreshing zing even today. The high/low, omnivorously scholarly essay in the hands of a fine modern writer (David Foster Wallace, say, yapping about "Hill Street Blues") is still dazzling. These first examples of the confluence of high and low culture, however, are full of gaffes that seem literally parodic now.

"I am strongly drawn to Camp, and almost as strongly offended by it. That is why I want to talk about it, and why I can," runs the opening of "Notes on 'Camp'". Well okay! What this means is that Ms. Sontag will be announcing that Aristophanes, who went in for fart jokes in a big way, is "in the pantheon of high culture", whereas the elegant Pope and the super-elegant Congreve are "camp." "To name a sensibility," she writes, "to draw its contours and to recount its history, requires a deep sympathy modified by revulsion."[26] Here is one of those wacky Frenchified misappropriations of

a regular word, in this case "revulsion," in a bid for Foucault-ish depth. Or Edward Lear-ish lunacy, take your pick.

"Most" Mozart— Camp, according to Sontag. But, Beethoven's quartets—pantheon of h.c. *Our Lady of the Flowers*—too "elevat-

flickr photo by greenmelinda, creative commons

ed" (!?) to be Camp. "The novels of Ronald Firbank and Ivy Compton-Burnett," on the other hand—Camp. In case the reader is not familiar with the novels of Ivy Compton-Burnett, they are full of the absolute wickedest people murdering babies and having incest on the q.t., while the novels of Ronald Firbank, featuring such characters as the King of Pisuerga getting "an impression of raised hats," really are camp as tits, which is a phrase I heard this Scotsman say one time. In any case, "Notes on 'Camp' " is a weirdly entertaining document, with far-out pronouncements like these cascading thick and fast throughout. Even a world-famous lefty like Sontag would never be able to get away with an un-PC whopper like the following nowadays (unsupported, like most of the assertions in "Notes on 'Camp'," by a single example or citation): "Jews and homosexuals are the outstanding creative minorities in contemporary urban culture [...] [t]he two pioneering forces of modern sensibility are Jewish moral seriousness and homosexual aestheticism and irony."

Undeniably, though, Sontag, like Mailer, wound up delivering a massive wallop of common sense to the academy simply by taking the whole of society as a fit subject for serious discourse. Unshackled from their first-class seats, intellectuals have been quite free to roam about the cabin of culture ever since. The comradely analysis of the beliefs and behavior of outsiders of all kinds was an incalculable boon to the quality and utility of American scholarship. It required some dorkismo to try it. And so, these then-young authors kind of deserved to get away with their almost totally senseless yammering about stuff that they did not understand, because they were breaking the most amazing new ground.

Both Mailer and Sontag went on to enjoy long careers of uninterrupted blabbing, most of it equally daft, and equally entertaining. But neither one ever really managed to shake the reactionary stance first assumed in those early years. Both flirted with filmmaking, journalism, politics and the stage, but neither ever had a success that quite fulfilled his early promise. The reason is not hard to find; the reactionary mind is an other-directed mind, not a balanced or original one. It seeks to refute the foolishness of the masses, to stake out a position higher than that of the common herd; but before this can be done, the coordinates of the common herd must be determined and then clambered up from, which renders the personal authenticity and interest of the whole project kind of moot. "Reactionary", you could say, is just about the opposite of "visionary." This is where the nascent dorkismo of Mailer and Sontag failed them; they both of them were trying a little too hard to be cool.

(Ťﬁřee.)

A number of today's far dorkier literary lions have largely been able to avoid this error, and the careers of a few already show signs of longer-lasting quality because of their amazing dorkismo. People still don't know what to make of Jonathan Franzen, for example, a terrific dork whose oft-mortifying personal candor is the equal of Mailer's, but whose moral and political positions are fraught with all sorts of interesting doubts, backtracking and self-abnegation. He is wedded to no dogma; watching him develop and grow in the public eye, one gets the impression of an always-doubting, questioning, curious mind, and most emphatically not an attention-seeking blowhard with a series of questionable axes to grind. Franzen's mind is both inner-directed, to the point where his awkwardness with the press almost defines his whole public persona, and other-directed enough to fuel his astonishing gifts of observation. Thus Franzen is constitutionally incapable of Maileresque preaching, and his withdrawn, uncompromising intellect won't permit much in the way of self-promotion, either, as was demonstrated by his chaotic run-in with Oprah Winfrey.

This episode was a masterpiece of dorkismo. For those who may have forgotten the details: shortly after Franzen's novel *The Corrections* was announced as a selection of Oprah's Book Club in the fall of 2001, the dorky author thoughtlessly expressed certain reservations in the *Portland Oregonian* and on the Powell's Books website about the Oprah Seal of Approval his book had just received. The device had already been printed on the dustjackets of tens of thousands of copies of *The Corrections,* in anticipation of Franzen's appearance on Oprah's Book Club:

The problem in this case is some of Oprah's picks. She's picked some good books, but she's picked enough schmaltzy, one-dimensional ones that I cringe, myself, even though I think she's really

Franzen: He is such a dork!

smart and she's really fighting the good fight. And she's an easy target.[27]

Oprah Winfrey responded to this with an imperial decree, icily canceling Franzen's appearance on her TV show:

> Jonathan Franzen will not be on The Oprah Winfrey Show because he is seemingly uncomfortable and conflicted about being chosen as an Oprah's Book Club selection. It is never my intention to make anyone uncomfortable or cause anyone conflict. We have decided to skip the dinner and we're moving on to the next book.

Now Franzen was pilloried in the press for his "arrogance," and so on, with the hand-wringing literary establishment bemoaning his lack of grace and *savoir-faire*. A few of us, however, were totally thrilled at Franzen's lack of *savoir-faire*. Plainly, no PR flack was advising this man on the "appropriate" thing to say in public. That his somewhat impolitic observations were also true to the meanest intelligence went practically unnoticed. He had simply said, so shockingly, just what he thought. That it was so shocking just goes to show how blandly stage-managed the world has sadly become. Have an opinion, go to jail!

The PR juggernaut of Oprah Winfrey, meanwhile, labored frantically to ensure that the talk-show queen emerged from this fracas with her shaky intellectual bona fides unscathed. A very few were heard to observe that Ms. Winfrey had behaved far more crassly than Franzen had, particularly in rescinding a dinner invitation because her prospective guest had dared to say that certain selections of Oprah's Book Club were "schmaltzy." Chris Lehmann wrote along these lines in *Slate:*

> But why is it, I wonder, that amid all the right-eous posturing over Jonathan Franzen's alleged elit-ism, no one has expended any critical scrutiny on Ms. Winfrey's particular haughty outburst? Here, after all, is a leading arbiter of public taste breaking off a brewing literary debate on grounds of prospec-tive discomfort and conflict. As a longtime book-worm (and let it be known, a good American fan of a great deal of mass culture), I had always taken con-flict and discomfort—and ambivalence, for that matter—to be robust signs of health in a cultural democracy. These chafing virtues are how literary debates (and kindred political ones) get settled. They are also how we remind ourselves that something serious is at stake in literary life—that it's not simply a healing anodyne for souls in various states of recovery, but something on which we can risk public disapproval, feuds, fallings out, even lawsuits.[28]

Where one had hoped that there would be an interesting televised discussion of High Culture vs. Low, the State of Literary Fiction in America Today, and so on, there was a teacup-sized tempest instead. Was the purpose of Oprah's Book Club to discuss and popularize literature—an activity which, presumably, would include airing a range of opinions—or to celebrate the "good taste" of its billionaire benefactress?

A few weeks after the dust-up, *The Corrections* won the National Book Award, by which time Franzen had apologized just flounderingly all over the place, and the whole thing eventually blew over.

I believe and hope that Jonathan Franzen will remain chockablock full of blundering dorkismo forever, like James Boswell did, and that he will never, ever turn into a speechifying blowhard and caricature of himself, the way so many literary lions have, but will instead continue to be completely inappropriate at least half the time and persist in blurting out every hopelessly compromising, deeply felt thing that pops into his capacious cranium.

Great Moments in Dorkismo, Vol. II

Rock and roll came down like a flood on the highbrows, because suddenly all these talented poets and visionaries were working in this "low" medium that no academic could care two pins about. But people who love art and music soon realized that genius was flowing there, and that you would be missing something so important, if you didn't know about it ... so that by now, it would be very hard to argue that Pound or Stevens have got a thing on Bob Dylan.

Lester Bangs, moralist, drug abuser and rock critic, surfed right down the front of that mighty cascade. He had such subtlety and wit, way more of those than any ordinary journalist had or ever would have, and he had brought it all to the rock and roll that we loved so much when we were teenagers in the 1970s, especially in the cracklingly impertinent pages of *Creem* (Boy Howdy!)

Lester Bangs what a dork and he changed American literature forever.

> Number one, everybody should realize that all this
> "art" and "bop" and "rock-'n'-roll" and whatever is
> all just a joke and a mistake, just a hunka foolishness
> so stop treating it with any seriousness or respect at
> all and just recognize the fact that its nothing but a
> Wham-O toy to bash around as you please in the
> nursery, its nothing but a goddam Bonusburger so
> just gobble the stupid thing and burp and go for the

Lester Bangs
1948–1982, via
Wikipedia

next one tomorrow; and don't worry about the fact that it's a joke and a mistake and a bunch of foolishness as if that's gonna cause people to disregard it and do it in or let it dry up and die, because it's the strongest, most resilient, most invincible Superjoke in history, nothing could possible destroy it ever, and the reason for that is precisely that it is a joke, mistake, foolishness. The first mistake of Art is to assume that it's serious. I could even be an asshole here and say that "Nothing is true; everything is permitted," which is true as a matter of fact, but people might get the wrong idea. What's truest is that you cannot enslave a fool.

—Lester Bangs, "James Taylor Marked for Death," collected in *Psychotic Reactions and Carburetor Dung*

King Dørk

Frank Portman (also affectionately known as "Dr. Frank") is the founder, songwriter and singer/guitarist of The Mr. T. Experience, a pop punk band formed in the mid-1980s in Northern California. MTX's songs spoke to a more thoughtful set of concerns than American punk bands, then as now composed mainly of half-baked anarchists, had hitherto embraced. The sound, attitude and especially the humor of MTX set the table for the likes of Green Day and Blink 182, who went on to global superstardom. Like Mike Scott, Tom Verlaine or Jeff Mangum, Frank Portman had a vision that found fame only in its echoing.

Some years later, Frank Portman wrote a novel, *King Dork;* an unendingly charming book, far more so than any Young Adult novel has any right to be. I happened onto it quite by accident, right when

I started thinking about writing this book, so that everything that said "dork" on it, I would go and check out. But I wound up being just dazzled by *King Dork,* and a lot of people seem to feel, as I do, that in this second career Dr. Frank is likely to achieve all the success that eluded him as a punk rocker.

The plot of *King Dork* is, among other things, a sly take on *The Catcher in the Rye.* It is the story of Tom Henderson, a typical fourteen-year-old high school outcast who detests high school, "normal" people and hypocrisy, and dreams of girls, liberty and rock and roll. He and his friend, fellow outcast Sam Hellerman, are starting a band whose name and logo change every few weeks.

Super Mega Plus
Guitar/Vox: Moelle
Bass, Prevarication, and Procuring Young Girls under
     False Pretenses: Sam Hell
Irregular Timekeeping: Brain-dead Panchowski
First Album: *A Woman Knows*

The Elephants of Style
Guitar: Mot Juste
Bass and Animal Husbandry: Sam Enchanted Evening
First Album: *Devil Warship*

Sentient Beard
Guitar/Vox: Mot Nosredneh
Bass and Upholstery: Samerica the Beautiful
First Album: *Off the Charts—Way Off*

Henderson hates his outsiderhood, while at the same time completely defining himself by it, in the time-honored manner of not only Holden Caulfield (whom Henderson also and especially hates,) but of young people everywhere. Henderson's war with the status quo has at times a bitterness that is at odds with the blithe, devil-may-care essence of the personality he is growing into, Portman seems to suggest. Adolescence is the time when most of us manage, or are forced, to negotiate the problem of fitting into the culture against the irresistible pull of our own nature. Few young people have yet grown sufficient stones to be themselves freely, no matter how fiercely they may long to do so.

Even though Frank Portman describes himself as having been a bit of a reactionary, growing up, we found him about as accepting and thoughtful as it's possible for a person to be. His take on dork matters was very illuminating to me and the Teenage Sidekick I brought along, who writes for her high school's music/culture rag, and who also loves *King Dork*. We were fortunate enough to inveigle Dr. Frank into coming out with us for soup dumplings in San Francisco, one lovely autumn morning.

   TS: I want to know about your band.

What about my band?

   MB: What were the other names, when did you start, and who was on Upholstery?

Basically it started when I was in college, like nineteen or twenty, like in the book, a lot of imaginary rock bands, and then sort of randomly, one of these imaginary bands recorded something for fun, or for a joke; we recorded at like the cheapest place we could find, then one of the guys made this decision that we would make it into a record. It was a joke for years, even though several of these little records were happening at the time, but we didn't play a lot. And eventually it was like twenty years of doing that, you know, without getting too far in show business, but we made little dents in popular culture in certain ways. You can exaggerate it, but it's not completely inaccurate to say that some of what we were doing influenced people who became famous, in a way. We set an example in the San Francisco area for people to do that kind of thing; when we were starting, the consensus was no, it is not popular to do that kind of thing. And then through sheer bloody-mindedness, sort of just because you weren't supposed to do it, you sort of do it anyway. And that is the animating spirit of punk rock: you don't know how to sing and you don't know how to play, and you don't know how to do anything and you might not even have any good instruments, but you do it anyway … that is pretty much the whole story.

And that is the story of my book as well, it seems really presumptuous to write a book, and I think that everybody pretty much would have predicted … I would have predicted it myself … I think that a good prediction would have been that I never would have finished it. Because I rarely finish anything, but a lot of people would have predicted that it wouldn't have gotten anywhere.

Both: @!(#>>?? Why do you say that?!

A lot of people try to write books and even if they are good they never get anywhere, never even get published or if they do, there's so much competition that nobody reads it, nobody buys it and then also: musicians writing novels. I think there's grounds for skepticism there. You know? But in the spirit of doing it anyway ...

MB: But you're a reader, clearly.

When I do appearances and I'm asked how I came to write a novel, I say that this is the first time I ever wrote a novel, but I have read *several*.

I wouldn't say I've read everything, you know, but I approached writing my book with the idea of wanting to reward readers for making the effort to read it, so I tried to make the reading of it fun, as much as possible.

Both: It IS fun.

I reflected on my past with reading, and I realized that there can be some really valuable, great things, but they can be so hard to fathom so that you don't feel like reading them, so they don't get read. So that's where my reading of other books was useful. I had never tried to write fiction before, ever, outside of songs.

MB: Tell me what the word "dork" means to you.

Maybe it's not the worst of all the things you get called when you're the non-mainstream type of personality, but I think there's a tendency, like there is with any derogatory term, to kind of take back the knife. Like, "We here, we're queer," or, "We're all bitches," or whatever you want to say. But by the time I was conscious of dorkiness, that had already happened, so it was something that you would choose to identify yourself with. Even so, it's almost like you could choose to ally yourself with a different tradition, develop a talent for it; I always thought of Tom Henderson really through my own very narrow version of existing, of thinking beyond the rah-rah, that "normal" is like the worst thing you could say about someone. But this idea—that you would say I'm kind of *dorky*, I'm a *dork*, I'm that kind of person, simultaneously it's kind of like saying I'm *special*, but it's also an indictment of the rest of society, for not being... for not being user-friendly to oneself.

Frank Portman, with Teenage Sidekick

MB: Tell me more about the outsider thing.

Again, I'm using my book to provide an example. In our popular culture, and maybe culture in general, particularly in the last century, there's an ideology of being a noble outsider; that's a thing that you really aspire to. And the symbol of that in my book, Holden Caulfield in *The Catcher in the Rye,* that that is a model to emulate ... I didn't have the same overwhelming association with *The Catcher in the Rye* that my character did, but there was a contradiction in that character and that attitude and that idea, of the antihero being something to emulate, which was taught in school and enforced by parents and priests and authority figures, what have you—that there is something valuable about being this kind of person, to kind of encourage you to think and identify with that figure; but then you have a situation where all the 'normal' people who are beating you up in the bathroom, you know, and humiliating the fat girl, or whatever, are also believing in this ideal of the outsider. And there is a weird disgust in there, and it inspires a degree of misanthropy, when you've lived through it; because actually, the supposed ideals that are being identified with contrast so sharply with the reality as it's lived; the teacher loves Holden Caulfield, but if there was a real Holden Caulfield there, they'd all be beating him up, and the teacher would be saying "Go, beat him up, beat him up beat him up!"

Then there's two sides, because in reality you are an outsider, and then you decide to cultivate it, and these things feed off each other; but you might come up with a different interpretation of outsiderhood from the one that the stream you're swimming against is based upon. That's how it gets ever more strange, the sorts of things you use to set yourself apart; rock music is a real easy way to do it, because you can value something for its obscurity, and that alone is an emblem of your specialness. And that's what I did, and that's what a lot of people do; you know, it's like a protest against the status quo that has an aesthetic content, but you could almost plug in just about anything as long as it's pure enough; although that's not how you experience it at the time, but stepping back from it and looking at it, that is what it is. You know, if I had gone to the kind of high school (which I didn't) but if I'd gone to sort of a hipper high school, where in 1981 all the cool kids were interested in punk rock (which did happen, though it didn't happen at my high school,) then punk rock would not have been what I would have gravitated toward. I don't know what I would have been into—maybe show tunes, who knows?!

When I was a kid, the whole idea of the dork in rock and roll had a kind of potency for me, when I was having my band in high school, I was never trying to pretend to be a sort of tough guy juvenile delinquent, kind of that *Lord of the Flies* kind of thing, but now, I go to high schools with my book and half the student body are hipsters with glasses…

MB: Like little Rivers Cuomoses.

Exactly! Before that mode became generalized, it was a lot more meaningful. I don't know what I would be doing if I was a high school student now, but I really doubt I would be … I would probably be shying away from that. You want to define yourself in a way that's not banal, you know, so how do you manage to do it, when there's been so many of the possibilities that your culture has already been experimenting with, until you get to the point where you figure out the right way to revive a previous subculture.

I find when I visit high schools now, and it does seem like as an adult coming back, you go there, and it seems like okay, well, you've got the kids with the green hair, you've got the kids with the horn-rimmed glasses… it's not as bad for being one of those kids as it used to be. And then you've got this fantasy, for me anyway, of going back, and if I was in high school I'd have all these friends, you know. But in reality—the punch line of bringing that up, is that then you talk to these individuals, we notice these types, identify them, "Oh, that guy is kinda like me," you talk to him, and he's *miserable*. And you're like, "What are you talking about?! You've got all this," and he's like everyone hates him, he hates society, he's about to kill himself. It's like there are experiences that do remain, it's still hard to the degree that it always was. This might be one of the reasons my book did strike a chord with teenagers, as well as with older people who remember all of that; looking at it from the inside rather than the outside, just describing it as something you're experiencing rather than as something you're observing, it's not that easy. I think that the experience of forming into a person is traumatic, no matter what.

MB: No matter what!

There are the girls who are the pretty, popular girls who have the eating disorders or whatever, they have got a nightmare world that from the outside you just can't—like, what the hell do they have to be worried about? They have everything that I didn't have when I was in high school!—but they've got something wrong. I mean, everyone has got something wrong—

Both: Yeah!

But when you're in it, you don't see that, and when you're trying to create a narrator of a novel, being balanced isn't what you want. You just want the narrow vision of this person, of this one experience.

MB: It's gonna hurt, the experience of becoming an individual is painful, even if you're in a really supportive, loving environment, but maybe it doesn't have to be AS painful.

Yeah, maybe not. A lot of people don't have as much difficulty. And I think a lot of the things that are self-reinforcing, like I certainly like the concept of not fitting into society more than I like the idea of fitting into it, even as I felt resentful about that; you talk about being against the stream, but then there are streams within streams, so there's a precocious rejection of the counterculture, for example the countercultural literature, because that was whoa, in fact I did pretend that I knew what the hell William Burroughs was talking about. So I had my moments of going with the flow, but mostly I had an aesthetic that was defined by opposition to whatever the status quo was. More often than not, the judgments that that led to were aesthetically right, but that's not due to me, the fact that I would prefer Dostoevsky to

William Burroughs, say, that I was so brilliant that I could recognize the reasons why—it's just that everyone was like, "Hey, you gotta read this book, man, it's *trippy*."

TS: I have this friend—aaagh! He LOVES William Burroughs. And you would really hate him! He is the biggest poser. You would like, kill him, there would be nothing left but three teeth and a belt buckle. And hipster sunglasses.

He's fourteen, and we've been friends since we were six, but now, it's like he can't be nice, ever, he has to be sooo cool … he has this whole crowd, he hangs out with the older cool indie kids ONLY.

That's very funny, that there's even "cool indie kids," I mean it's interesting how the categories shift. It didn't exist when I was in high school.

TS: Oh yeah, they're all, anything you like, like for instance, the Aquabats suck, but you know who's cool the PIXIES, and that's ALL, that's all you should listen to.

You always have that. With my band as an example, you know, this attitude of punk rock, and then indie-pop, post-punk, whatever the hip kind of music was, and within that there's punk rock with its stubborn refusal to die, punk rock, and that's a stream that you could swim against, and in fact that's what my band did. The genre that my band is associated with is called pop punk. And to people that are 'real' punks, that was always this big thing, that was partly motivated by these people that are going around pretending to be these tough guys, and they got all their political songs... and we were like "oh, we're going to play love songs."

And so it was all opposition to *something*, and that's how culture is created. Rock and roll really did create an efficient context for those for-and-against battles to rage with the popular culture, but any art milieu is like that, you experience it firsthand when you're sixteen, and then read about the Symbolists, or riots at the Stravinsky performance, and there's a consistent dynamic.

[Of soup dumplings]: Yeah, this is like the best thing I ever had. I can't believe I went 42 years without having it.

The pattern of objecting to something because it's the status quo dies hard, even if there's not good reasons for it. I always wonder if I'd grown up in a different sort of environment—

MB: Where was this?

I was born in San Francisco, and my parents moved to the suburbs when I was school age, in the Peninsula. The environment where I was raised was very regulation sort of suburban California liberal culture, my parents were kind of Martin Luther King liberals, and Catholics—that Liberation Theology kind of Catholicism. If I'd been raised in a different situation, as they were, which sort of formed their leftiness, I would have maybe ended up different, gone to a different college; but you realize, not that you can change it, but a pattern of sort of assuming that playing the role of the devil's advocate is obviously the superior role in any situation; that doesn't go away, and it creates some paradoxical situations. For instance, I don't live in Berkeley but it might as well be Berkeley, and that impulse leads you down some pretty interesting paths, which would be different if you lived in Dallas, or whatever. Everywhere is not Berkeley.

5ophistication and its discontents

(one.)

If to be hip means to know what is *au courant* from what is "so five minutes ago"—to have the highest, strictest standards for such things—then necessarily, the less you love, the better you are. It's pretty sterile and even destructive to have pickiness be the central feature of your psyche, and yet this is the default setting for millions of young Americans.

Worse still, anybody who is fool enough to love or believe in or even mean anything at all is currently liable to be attacked by some would-be ironist asking, in mingled pity and surprise, "oh, really, you *like* that?" Notice too, how it requires zero taste or knowledge to engage in that low pastime; it only needs a stagy little eruption of bile.

A lot has been written about the national epidemic of irony—even in the most exalted literary circles, where the snotty refusal to like anything has put enough of a kibosh on good criticism that when Heidi Julavits wrote about it, she created such a brouhaha that the word 'snark' shot into general currency like a rocket, and it's stayed there ever since.

Julavits began by insisting that we pity the poor critic:

> George Orwell, in his essay "Confessions of a
> Book Reviewer," postulates a Sisyphean vision of the
> average book critic, a pouchy-eyed and preternaturally
> geriatric fiction writer clad in grubby robe and slip-
> pers, cowering behind a vertical thatch of cigarette
> butts and gazing at a mail packet of five novels, about
> which he's meant to write an 800 word review by
> noon the following day. This coal laborer of the intel-
> lectual set has made his living turning "tripe" into cul-
> tural fossil fuels, he has sacrificed his standards for "a
> glass of inferior sherry," and the effects, Orwell warns,
> are dismally incapacitating.[29]

This was a very influential piece despite the incredible
phrase, "postulates a Sisyphean vision." Oh boy, I still do not
get that cigarette-butt décor scheme whatsoever. Why vertical? And if they're vertical, how can they be thatch? And why
is he "cowering behind" said improbable thatch? It's such a
mess. You can't turn tripe into petroleum, cultural or otherwise! Maybe she ought to have worked 'à la mode de Caen' in
there somehow, instead. No I'm kidding, I'm kidding. In any
case, this article was so influential because, after a tough slog
through a whole lot of sludge, we arrive at this:

> I don't know what many critics believe when it
> comes to literature; at worst, I fear that book reviews
> are just an opportunity for a critic to strive for

humor, and to appear funny and smart and a little bit bitchy, without attempting to espouse any higher ideals—or even to try to understand, on a very localized level, what a certain book is trying to do, even if it does it badly. This is wit for wit's sake—or, hostility for hostility's sake. This hostile, knowing, bitter tone of contempt [...] I call it Snark, and it has crept with alarming speed into the reviewing community.

Underneath all that cultural petroleum-tripe, or whatever, there was an actual reader clamoring for books to be read and understood—not just sneered at—and well, everybody pretty much just sat up and shouted, "ENGAGE!"

If the piñata of approval is to be lifted every time somebody takes a swing at it, nobody is going to be getting any candy, and how tiresome is that? It is very, very tiresome. One hears people complaining about their own irony and anhedonia almost nonstop; there were 61,400 Google hits on the phrase "tired of irony" just now. As opposed to "tired of ironing," which is what Oliver thought I said, weighing in at a mere 3,740 hits, and most of those in the form of a question posed by hopeful drycleaners. Which suggests that Americans are at this moment at least 20 times more tired of irony than they are of ironing (I know I am, and I loathe ironing!) Or, to learn what Americans think of their ironical *cognoscenti*, you can go to urbandictionary.com, look up 'hipster,' and experience the sorrows of a generation.

2. Hipster

Listens to bands that you have never heard of. Has hairstyle that can only be described as "complicated." (Most likely achieved by a minimum of one week not washing it.) Probably tattooed. Maybe gay. Definitely cooler than you. Reads Black Book, Nylon, and the Styles section of the New York Times. Drinks Pabst Blue Ribbon. Often. Complains. Always denies being a hipster. Hates the word. Probably living off parents money - and spends a great deal of it to look like they don't have any. Has friends and/or self cut hair. Dyes it frequently (black, white-blonde, etc. and until scalp bleeds). Has a closet full of clothing but usually wears same three things OVER AND OVER (most likely very tight black pants, scarf, and ironic tee-shirt). Chips off nail polish artfully after $50 manicure. Sleeps with everyone and talks about it at great volume in crowded coffee shops. Addicted to coffee, cigarettes (Parliaments, Kamel Reds, Lucky Strikes, etc.), and possibly cocaine. Claims to be in a band. Rehearsals consist of choosing outfits for next show and drinking PBR. Always on the list. Majors or majored in art, writing, or queer studies. Name-drops. May go by "Penny Lane," "Eleanor Rigby," etc. when drunk. On PBR. Which is usually.

I am not a fucking hipster! (sweeps bangs to side dramatically and takes a swig of PBR)

tags hip coffee queer pabst hair
by penny rigby capitol hill, seattle, wa May 28, 2006 email it

(Twø.)

They're the coolest kids in school—foul-mouthed, bored, mean, anarchic, glossily sophisticated, forever faux-lamenting their substance abuse—and still you kind of like hanging out with them, because they can be hilarious. Especially when they are going on about the finale of "The Sopranos":

> RHYMES WITH STORY: It was a little Six Feet Under for me!
> BALK BTW: I was glad — at the very least — that there wasn't that Six Feet kind of montage-over-whispery-female-vocal bullshit at the end. Although the choice of Journey was completely unforgiveable [sic] and the real reason people should be mad at Chase […]
> RHYMES WITH STORY: If you're going to hate on

Journey, we're going to have REAL PROBLEMS.
That particular tableau was a tribute to America.
BALK BTW: Oh, don't get me started on America.
RHYMES WITH STORY: Well, if you hate Journey,
you hate America.
BALK BTW: Yes and yes.
RHYMES WITH STORY: Well!
BALK BTW: AJ: More or less annoying?
RHYMES WITH STORY: AJ totally redeemed as a
LITTLE BITCH. I mean, what the——. What a mon-
ster. He's yer America.
BALK BTW: Exactly.

After a while, though, you can't help but get kind of bored
with the all-hate, all-the-time thing.

**The Internet Sucks: Magazine Reading for Lazy
Idiots**

**An 'n+1' Party: "It Turns Out That In Order To
Become An Intellectual, You Must First Become A
Pseudo-Intellectual" … (It is always so helpful when
friends of authors whose books you didn't like
explain why said books are good!)**

**Hope Atherton and Elise Overland, accompanied by
one fucking retarded scarf**

**Oh, the irony of miniature Bud cans…in the Prada
Store**

You decide: is Hamish Bowles the Harry Potter or Frodo of fashion?

Glenn O'Brien, obviously happy to be alive and wearing a tartan sleeping bag.

'Debutard' Tinsley Mortimer shares her thoughts about the works of Marx and Engels. PSYCH! The Post has no idea what the word 'socialist' means, and Tinsley Mortimer gives the most retarded quotes imaginable. Seriously, *more retarded than you are currently imagining them to be.*

Gawker ("daily Manhattan media news and gossip. Reporting live from the center of the universe") is a temple, in blog form, to the twitchy but invincible self-esteem of New York "media professionals." They'll go after anybody who can be made to look foolish—journalists, starlets, moguls, politicians. But *Gawker's* writers are so lacking in actual beliefs, passions or even mild convictions of their own that their rare display of enthusiasm comes off really mawkish and obtuse in just the manner they're slagging the other 99.97% of the time. It takes forever to find a favorable mention of anything whatsoever in there, but here they are, half-recommending Cormac McCarthy's "gruesomely violent" *Blood Meridian:*

> Imagine Biblical resonance and lyricism with
> access to a dictionary-thesaurus created by redneck
> savants of the period, yet somehow constructed with

Western austerity and concrete detail. Few readers
have an indifferent reaction to *Blood Meridian*, as
you will either devour it in a day or toss it aside after
ten pages. If you do get into it, you will thank us.
Profusely.[30]

"Redneck savants," no kidding. If anybody else had written these unfortunate lines, no doubt the *Gawker* crew would
"somehow" have gone after their sorry author with an
icepick. Also, how lukewarm is this recommendation? Could
they hold McCarthy any farther away from themselves without dropping him into the ravine???

And so alas for America's intelligentsia, who have
Forgotten How to Love. And to such a foolish purpose!—
they apparently want everyone to know how hip they are, and
how nothing is good enough for them. Well, fine, okay, nothing is good enough for them. So what? The sole result of that
is a twisted form of repression that they themselves really
hate, along with everything else that they hate.

Because if nothing is good enough to enjoy freely, then
pleasure itself is verboten. This is a super-no-fun policy, so it's
no surprise that no hipster wants to be called a hipster. Even
though one of the great tenets of hipsterism is a studied repu-
diation of repression (because repression most often means
sexual repression, or teetotalling, and hipsters want no part of
that stuff,) hipsterism turns out to be the most stultifying
intellectual position there is; and the most-hip hipsters, like
the staff of *Gawker*, find themselves obliged to forbid themselves to enjoy, appreciate or believe anything whatsoever.

In other words, the hipsters are suffering from a kind of

reverse-earnestness that is in fact as old as the hills. It's a very, very stubborn malady. The phrase "weary ironizing" showed up in a letter Martin Heidegger wrote to Hannah Arendt in 1925:

> Someday, anyone with any blood and passion left inside will necessarily get sick of this inside-out, old man's "earnestness" ... and then will also avoid the equally contorted opposite extreme of weary ironizing – now *that* really is futility. (Arendt, Hannah and Martin Heidegger. *Letters 1925–1975.* New York, Harcourt, 2003)

(*Herr Professor* Heidegger, you have had a long wait!)

The second, more significant result of having Forgotten How to Love is that criticism has betrayed half its purpose; critics are supposed to discourage the bad, yes, but also to encourage the good. And so little ever is or can be reckoned good that our whole intelligentsia has been bled white and frozen solid.

The genius who best articulated the solution to these problems was the late, lamented dork, David Foster Wallace.

(Ťȟřєє.)

David Foster Wallace, the Dork Lord of American Letters

The most sizzling star in the American literary firmament did not hesitate to inform us that he was called "Slug" in junior high. When interviewed by Charlie Rose on TV, he wore his

"I heard all kinds of sneery stuff about the book Bridges of Madison County *when it came out, and joined in the sneering, and then saw the movie version on an airplane and bawled my head off at the end, which was mortifying."*
—*David Foster Wallace in* Amherst *magazine, Spring 1999*

gruesome "signature" bandana tied round his head, a too-small shirt, and a tie. He sweat a lot, he said. He was scared of bugs and rollercoasters. The good-natured ease with which David Foster Wallace displayed his painfully human frailties won him the comradely love of his public in a way that Cormac McCarthy's steely manliness or Don DeLillo's elegant hand-wringing never could, though these latter appear to be men of fine character and are easily as influential, as American literary icons go. I'm not even getting into Wallace's generosity of spirit here, or his whopping gifts as a prose stylist. Just because he was such a dork, Wallace confounded the 20th-century notion of the Western intellectual as an aloof, superior and phlegmatic character.

And there was more, so much more, to Wallace's dorkismo. He was kind, and goofily, distinctively erudite, and very, very funny, though with a mind so keen and full that this gentlest of men was also, not to put too fine a point on it, capable of really terrifying causticity. But most of all, he was our most skilled and valiant champion against the irony and ennui that have crippled American culture. I'll be calling this whole tendency "ironism," Richard Rorty's coinage. He defined the ironist this way:

> 1. She has radical and continuing doubts about the final vocabulary she currently uses, because she has been impressed by other vocabularies, vocabularies taken as final by people or books she has encountered;
> 2. She realizes that argument phrased in her present vocabulary can neither underwrite nor dissolve these doubts;
> 3. Insofar as she philosophizes about her situation, she does not think that her vocabulary is closer to reality than others, that it is in touch with a power not herself.[31]

This is careful, technically phrased philosophical work,

but what it also boils down to is exactly the same old "hipster" business I've just been railing against. Rorty was professionally precise about this real thing that we're living with all the time. [An aside: Can I just rail, also, against the academy's irritating and still-current practice of referring to any random "someone" as "she," which is just absurd because, about half the time, such a person is necessarily "he." Academy: how about if you're a girl you have to write "he," and if you're a boy, you write "she"? This would be fair, and get your superannuated point across without giving the annoying impression that at some point in the late 20th c., the place suddenly became overrun with females.]

Okay ... you know that old saw advising against wrestling a pig? So in this analogy, ironism was the pig and Wallace the wrestler; and as in the old saw, there was a danger of mistaking the wrestler for the pig, for both were bound to wind up covered in mud, and fed up. Careless readers saw an ironist in Wallace himself. But in time, it will become clear that Wallace had in fact managed to lay that pig down, and pretty much sat on him for the duration. There were other and worse beasts that he did not fare so well against.

> The next real literary "rebels" in this country
> might well emerge as some weird bunch of anti-rebels,
> born oglers who dare somehow to back away from
> ironic watching, who have the gall actually to endorse
> and instantiate single-entendre principles. Who treat
> of plain old untrendy human troubles and emotions
> in U.S. life with reverence and conviction. Who
> eschew self-consciousness and hip fatigue.[32]

"Good People," Wallace's last published story in the *New Yorker* (February 5th, 2007) was deliberately simple, kind of a crack across the jaw to those who had kept on blasting him for his famous opacity; the story has no footnotes, none of the nervous tics of Wallace's natural prose style (I say "natural" because he generally wrote very very much the way he spoke, and behaved, which was as if his consciousness were alive in front of you like a hive of bees and each bee had its own specific task, or footnote, it was working on. He was a distracted guy but with an unnervingly focused way of looking at you, and of hearing unerringly what people meant, rather than only what they said.) This story, one of the last he ever published, was an absolute instantiation of "single-entendre principles," indicating that in addition to his many other virtues, he put his money where his mouth was.

Gifted, happening writers are pretty much obliged to take on the current cultural bugbears, so it's no surprise that Wallace spent a lot of effort protesting against consumerism, capitalist greed and empty-headed ironizing, as many of his colleagues have likewise done. Being the dork of all time, Wallace was able to cut to the heart of ironism's sterility like no other, before or since:

> Irony's useful for debunking illusions, but most
> of the illusion-debunking in the U.S. has now been
> done and redone. Once everybody knows that equal-
> ity of opportunity is bunk and Mike Brady's bunk
> and Just Say No is bunk, now what do we do? All
> we seem to want to do is keep ridiculing the stuff.
> Postmodern irony and cynicism's become an end in

itself, a measure of hip sophistication and literary savvy. Few artists dare to try to talk about ways of working toward redeeming what's wrong, because they'll look sentimental and naive to all the weary ironists. Irony's gone from liberating to enslaving.

The real trouble with ironism is not that it's boring, or lazy (because it's the cheapest possible way of attempting to make yourself look smart.) It's that ironism keeps you from caring about anything. This is not an inconsequential problem, it's literally a deadly one. It would make you leave Viktor Laszlo for dead in Casablanca. It would stop you from caring who the hell is president enough to get your sorry behind to the voting booth. Wallace provided the best articulation of this danger in American letters.

Still more valuably, Wallace himself cared so much about the things he did care about that he dorkily cleared the path toward the very solution this book was written to promote. He didn't just write with dorkismo, he lived it. Nothing was too weird or trivial or too low for him, and although he was by far the trendiest, most recherché, most difficult American novelist of our time (which people are still all ooh, ahh if you say you love *Infinite Jest,* because it is a seriously hard book,) he was also the most ridiculous dork who was ready to give free rein to an obsessive interest in anything, really anything—tennis, John McCain, lobsters, pleasure cruises, right-wing radio, David Lynch—and thereby liberated many a scholarly dork to follow his own personal inclinations, however out-there those might be. And thereby gave the rest of us license to examine and entertain freely the whole panorama of the world, unconstrained by any arbiters of taste or worth outside those whom we might wish to consult ourselves, for our own purposes. And thereby, and thereby. He set a lot of balls rolling, one way and another.

Paradoxically, though, actually caring about things can make you appear snotty in much the same way in which ironists are snotty, so that Wallace could sometimes seem incredibly, horribly snotty. The man with convictions has no real use for those who lack them. Conviction demands solid *rejection*, the rejection of ideas or principles that betray or fall short, and Wallace came to maturity among the PC academic crowd who had come to know nothing outside of their own bland "tolerance" of everything but conviction itself, and their "weary ironizing;" they'd lost not only the ability to love or believe, but the ability to *reject*, not even beginning to get anywhere near a predisposition to become fiercely pissed off in defense of deeply held principles.

To the man with convictions, an ironist is barely even alive. Pity and condescension for that half-state can't help but follow. Contempt, even, when you can see that there's a real person in there who is just going diametrically the wrong way, lemminglike, for no reason. When Wallace showed contempt (and he did, a lot,) he did it to show not how little he cared, but involuntarily, because of how much. So he could be terribly cutting, but that was because he was "involved in mankind," and not because he wanted other people to be scared of him.

Take something as seemingly trivial as his attention to English grammar, as described by one of his students, Zack Schenkkan:

He was obsessed with grammar. He wrote about it some, especially in one published essay, but it's hard to understand the depth of his obsession without having written and turned in papers to him. Responding to the first essay I ever turned into him, Dave started with the line, "There are a lot of interesting themes you've touched on ... but to discuss those themes would be like conversing about the weather over a bloody, mutilated corpse."[33]

So wow, that's sounding pretty snotty, and not so tactful; but it's obvious to those who are at all familiar with his work (even just the 'published essay' in question, "Tense Present: Democracy, English and the Wars over Usage", which appeared in *Harper's* in April 2001,) that he really, really wanted Zack Schenkkan to care, as he himself did, so much, about doing it right; hence the rather barbaric put-down. He was like that a lot, Swiftian in his "savage indignation." Even w/r/t grammar.

But whoever doubts Wallace's essential dorkiness and kindness, well, maybe you could read my notes from his reading in January 2006 at the Hammer Museum in Los Angeles. I wrote this for a group of Wallace admirers online.

This one young guy asked Wallace to comment on the role of religion in his life; the piece Wallace had read focuses on his posse at church, on 9/11, when he was living in Bloomington IN. Wallace then asked this kid to comment on the role of religion in his own life, so that he would be able to answer the question effectively, "because either I don't answer it at all, or I answer for three hours, which is obviously not practical." And this kid said, well, I go to church, but am not super-dogmatic about the sort of doctrinal part; he considers himself very skeptical. "What is the role of it in your life, if you're skeptical?" counters Wallace. "Well ... it's a community, and like most of my friends are like these, well, liberal lefties [crowd giggles appreciatively at self-deprecating but also slightly defiant tone of kid, when I suddenly realize that this politics is probably about the only universally shared characteristic of the audience], and there are all kinds of people at my church, and I think it's important to know as many people as I can, who ... well, I just think it's important to know all kinds of people." And Wallace said really gently, "Now look, I am not being the slightest bit sarcastic AT ALL when I just say .... 'Ditto.'"

And I asked a question (Brawner held up his hand for me, because I'm too short to be seen in such a crowd, even whilst bouncing) about l'affaire Frey ("can you comment, please.") He launches in, "you know, what it made me feel was really old—I say this because I can see you are a lot younger than I am," and I yell out because they'd just taken the microphone, "Noooo, I am older than you!" (like just over a year, I think) and he goes, "well then, you are wickedly well-preserved," which, though it sounds perilously like "fossilized" I was very very flattered by it, I must say. The answer was excellent, subtle, and could be decocted into his phrase, "a line has been crossed"—to indicate that readers can indeed be (perhaps in this case have been) betrayed, no matter how grey the area between memoir and fiction has become.

One question about Vollman he answered with a lovely anecdote. First a little rambling about yes, I admire Vollman, and his book was fantastic, more fantastic than I hoped it would be, but (to the questioner) don't say anything to him about that; "He is an expert shot." He went on to explain that he and Vollman had both been invited to read once at CBGB, and Vollman went first. And Vollman in his reading passed out X-rays to the crowd, and fired a revolver (loaded with blanks) into the air. "And then it was my turn, and I [makes voice smaller and more childlike] read a Poem." O he is such a hoot. He said he was rather in awe of the powers of research of both Vollmann and Powers. "Vollmann is the guy who has himself parachuted into the Arctic to get material."

Then there was this totally lame kind of art-museum matron who was on about her book group, and she was explaining how Wallace uses all these Hard Words, and did he make them up, these words like for masturbation, and Wallace said very innocently (he does a fine Innocent Look, does Wallace, it's positively altar boy), "Can you give me an example?" and she goes, "Priapic" (a hard word if ever I heard one ho ho) which is so totally embarrassing because it is such a common word that has nothing to do with masturbation, and so indeed, Wallace gave a long reply including the remark, "'Priapic' refers to an uncontrolled and irresolvable erection," which got a huge laugh. He said something about wondering how come that was so funny, which I could have told him straightaway, it was the word 'irresolvable' that was the so, so totally Wallacian word choice with its slight sadness and perplexity. At the end, he spoke maybe my favorite phrase of the night: "'Priapic' I think is a word that's in a lot of people's arsenal, in today's America."

The really weird thing was that some of those present at the reading wrote afterwards that Wallace had been contemptuous of the boy who had asked him about religion, which if only you could have seen the soft, gentle, kind way in which he said, "ditto." This principled dork had absolutely no use for pretension, but he was ready to respect any and all sincerity—what he used to call "authenticity"—no matter where it came from or how clumsily it was put forward. You see how easily these things can get so confused! But if you just view it through the dorkismic lens, and are ready to embrace all sincerity, certain thorny questions become clear and simple.

There was a really good and sad illustration of all these points from Wallace's Pomona colleague, Sean Pollack:

> Even though I worked at Pomona during his time there and taught in the English Department for a year, I'm sorry to say I did not know him well. But

I did know a bit of his work, and had known of him since the mid 1990s when all of my friends were urging to me to read *Infinite Jest*. I had no interest in his big books when they came out - I found the whole gen-X/irony thing a little toxic, even though he was not part of the problem. However, I did come to enjoy much of his non-fiction, and I did teach his essay "Democracy, English and the Wars over Usage" for a History of the English language class.

I heaped a teaspoon of scorn on the illogic of one or two of his more prescriptivist tendencies (my main point concerned the problem with evolutionary narratives about language). Then I went and looked up the source of the epigram [sic] of the article: "Dilige, et quod vis, fac." This is commonly translated as "love, and do what you will" […] *Diligere* means something like love/diligence - giving a damn, basically. And the source is Augustine's sermon on 1 John 7-8.

For me, this key passage from that source bespeaks what I imagine was Wallace's approach to teaching, writing, and the very language:

Once for all, then, a short precept is given you: Love, and do what you will: whether you hold your peace, through love hold your peace; whether you cry out, through love cry out; whether you correct, through love correct; whether you spare, through love do you spare: let the root of love be within, of this root can nothing spring but what is good.

> Following a trail left by Wallace's use of that aphorism led me to see him in a different way altogether: Not the self-described language-"snoot," but one who never forgot that love of language is the basis of all that is and should be done in writing, teaching, and even "correction."[34]

This obviously really smart guy who'd worked right alongside Wallace—even he had managed to mistake Wallace for a fashionably "toxic" ironist. Prof. Pollack seems to have disliked the arch, playful way that Wallace had about him, as maybe evidenced by his refusal to cite the grammar essay "Tense Present" by its whole, true name. But then he got to thinking about it more.

If you honor Prof. Pollack's view (and I do,) that what Wallace did really was done out of love (though I would characterize Wallace's idea of that "love" as embracing far more than language), then his remark about the "bloody, mutilated corpse" appears like a joke, hyperbole, the deliberate insistence on an absurd exaggeration in order to show both caring, and a playful consciousness that it is really silly, to care that much. How could anyone capable of all those subtle things forbear from speaking his own language, just because some people might have misunderstood?

The "mass culture critique," which is a highfalutin' phrase coined by colossally annoying *Partisan Review* editor Dwight Macdonald to mean your basic self-congratulatory highbrowism, is still all too prevalent out there. It's a weird irony that Wallace was so opposed to this thing that he was forever accused of himself. Still, in the last few years, a lot has changed. Writers like Wallace himself have done much to show the way toward a real cultural democracy.

But as much as he wanted to go to church and hang out with his high-school friends in the Midwest and know and write about all kinds of people, Wallace's writing is generally difficult, and he was inescapably learned, a "highbrow" in spite of himself. By the end of his life (for example, in "Good People," which turned out to be an excerpt from *The Pale King*, the novel he never finished) he was fighting highbrowism with all he had, and had he lived he might have figured out a way to write stuff that anybody could read and that would still be interesting and satisfying to him. He didn't want to be the prisoner of his intellect, didn't want to be defined or limited by all that went with that. He didn't want to Forget How to Love. It's so easy to be overwhelmed by his brilliance that you overlook the fact that he had been looking for, and finding, another, dorkier way.

The new puritans

(øne.)

Alexis de Tocqueville was a big fan of the early Puritans. He thought their doctrine provided the American template for ideal behavior, and predicted that that template would long endure. He was right, as usual.

The Puritans believed our world to be desperately flawed, and that the responsibility of repairing it confers on each of us an obligation to self-control and right action. They had an exacting code of beliefs that involved setting a sky-high standard for personal conduct, and then living by it, and demanding that others live by it also.

Little enough has changed, alas, that the aspects of American Puritanism that Tocqueville admired—thoughtful, industrious, and egalitarian—are still a positive and appropriate response to our damaged world, whether you want to refer to the damage as "sin," as the Puritans did, or just agnostically observe what a mess things are in. Their values have been transformed again and again, but the early Puritans are still providing the bedrock of what it wouldn't be so far wrong to call the American character.

The Greatest Generation was a prime example of this. Among the many lingering voices of that age—Frank Capra, Howard Hawks, Sloan Wilson, William Gaddis, William H. Whyte, Ernest Hemingway—there's a common recognition of the need for absolute personal responsibility, the obligation to work hard, be honest, try for excellence, care for the weak, fight and take real risks for your beliefs, restrain the selfish impulse. These were core American beliefs, Puritan in origin, that any atheist could (and did) subscribe to. (For more on this, see James Morone's *Hellfire Nation* and, in a hilarious WWII send-up, Max Shulman's *The Feather Merchants*.)

Decreasingly sustained by that shared sense of personal responsibility, Puritanism has suffered a long, slow decline into the emptied-out sophistications of our own day. What does discernment even mean, outside the framework of a responsible sense of the human condition? Not so much, maybe. Without a moral imperative to keep us on our toes, "high standards" devolve into mere games of one-upmanship: who has the most? Who knows what's what? Who can get the best table, and who was there first?

Alexis de Toqueville, proto-dork
(via Wikimedia Commons)

There's a flip side to Puritan austerity that we've inherited intact, though, the side that gave those early American moralists such a bad name; judgmental, witch-burning, pleasureless and full of hate. For today's version of Puritanical holier-than-thou, cf. the "superiority" that can find little more to demand than entrée into the latest nightclub. Today's Puritans won't dance any more than the seventeenth-century ones did—not because it's sinful or frivolous, but because they're too cool for it. But the same principle is at work in both cases; a sense of superiority to our fellow men that forbids indulgence in their low pleasures. The castigating side of the Puritan character is alive and well; there is very little to choose between the orthodoxy of Cotton Mather and that of *Gawker;* thin-lipped, disapproving, pouncing on the tiniest infraction, complaining and hating elevated to a whole way of life. This is so even if the worst "sin" you can think of is to live in a suburban tract house.

(Dorks, it need hardly be said, are entirely impervious to any of that nonsense, because they don't care where we are having lunch or where your parents are from, and they are all ready to dance like a big spaz. Right now!! And better yet, more spazzily than you! With the added benefit of making you look graceful by comparison.)

So, are we deciding how to behave, or not behave, based on ethical or moral convictions; or by the operation of taste, an aesthetic sensibility; or have we got some other kind of ambition? We like to think we've transcended these old-fashioned imperatives, but I submit that we are just not getting how we're being conned, here. We're trading away a rational sense of purpose and not getting anything for it but solipsism and ennui. Don't worry, I'm not going to tell you to go off and become Amish, or anything. Much as I love those hats! Just, I think it would be good to know what we're up to.

෧

(T̆w̥ø̥.)

Clement Greenberg was a famous American art critic who started off his career by sneering at *hoi polloi* in very much the modern manner. In the incredibly lame essay "Avant-Garde and Kitsch," which appeared in *Partisan Review* in 1939, he wrote:

> Superior culture is one of the most artificial of all human creations, and the peasant finds no "natural" urgency within himself that will drive him toward Picasso in spite of all difficulties. In the end the peasant will go back to kitsch when he feels like looking at pictures, for he can enjoy kitsch without effort.[35]

Astonishingly, this essay is still cited, and frequently. I suspect that half this stuff stays famous simply because nobody ever goes back and actually reads it. In any case, Greenberg was then thirty, and he would be laying down the aesthetic law for the next half-century.

Nowadays it would be almost impossible to use the phrase "superior culture" outside of quotation marks—and even less, to reflect airily on the putative views of "the peasant"—but in those days Americans still believed in an impenetrable barrier between high and low. They may also have been worried about exactly who "the peasant" might be, and hoping it wasn't them.

In retrospect, Greenberg's deficiencies loom large, though a lot of contemporary artists and critics still admire his work. His narrow definition of "only the best" would ensure that he missed the Pop Art boat by a mile, in addition to a fleet of other seaworthy vehicles. He was contemptuous of the high-art value of Hollywood movies, a position that would be pretty laughable today. Greenberg (along with the rest of the *Partisan Review* gang) may have dictated what would count as "superior culture" with a view to improving American tastes and habits, but because he approved of so little—and because he couldn't bear anything that the peasant might be into—he could only narrow, and never widen, those tastes. In other words, because they were so very, very concerned about appearing to be the tastefullest guys in town, these critics suffered from a terrible deficiency of dorkismo. They sound kind of lonely and troubled to today's ear, which is just a little more attuned to clarity, friendliness and approachability than to "authority." That's why it was such a blast of fresh air when Mailer and Sontag arrived on the scene. They appeared to be living in the world, rather than just sniffily observing it.

Rather than attempting to fit his professional convictions into an integrated worldview, as modern critics would later do, Greenberg dictated exclusively from on high. Surprisingly, as it happens, he'd done well to put as much distance as possible between himself and his audience, because alas! the poor guy was built far more along peasant lines than drawing-room ones. A drunken, brawling maniac who at age five beat a goose to death with a shovel,[36] he kind of went on from there to become a one-man Praetorian Guard for the testosterone-fueled Abstract Expressionists, starting with fellow drunken, brawling maniac Jackson Pollock. Not that he wasn't talented; Greenberg was and is deified for his taste and, even just looking at photos of his New York apartment, there can be no doubt he had that. Indeed he is no-longer-living proof that exquisite taste and exquisite manners do not necessarily go hand in hand; he was famous, maybe most famous, for going around and belting people at cocktail parties. It's hard to fathom how anybody who could behave in this way could also have found himself *elegantiae arbiter.* There was a freaky schism between the rarefied judgment and the furious way of life. A *poser* schism. Greenberg was one of the earliest 20th-century critics to pith the American character of its spiritual core; one of the first of the uptight, impossible-to-please *cognoscenti.*

As we have been saying, a lot of today's critics likewise resort, in what is really an old-fashioned way, to sneering in place of thoughtfulness; the same kind of "no" is waiting to spring out as the default response to everything. A thick root of this tendency springs up from the pages of *Partisan Review,* once America's premier bastion of highbrow snottiness and surprisingly influential, considering the fact that hardly anybody ever read it. In 2004, when it finally ceased publication, career highbrow Sven Birkerts wrote that in its heyday, *Partisan Review* was "a model of mattering."[37] No, not nattering! "Mattering."

Clement Greenberg's editor at *Partisan Review* was the cultural critic and breathtakingly conceited loon Dwight Macdonald. James Wolcott wrote in the *New York Times* on the centenary of Macdonald's birth:

> In 1980, Skidmore College was the site of a conference on the sunny topic "American Civilization:

Failure in the New World?" […] [Macdonald's] foil on the panel was *The New Republic's* eternal film critic, Stanley Kauffmann, the gentlemanly soul of generosity, who at one point said he didn't want to speak slightingly of "the popcorn crowd," which made Macdonald crack, "Aw, go ahead." Kauffmann: "No, no; Ingmar Bergman has remarked that those who go to see a Doris Day film — forgive me, is she still alive? — may go to see one of his films the following week. Often in the same theater." Macdonald: "They shouldn't be allowed to." Back and forth they bantered, like a couple of cranky pigeons on a park bench, until Kauffmann explained to the audience that Macdonald came from the Mencken generation, more comfortable responding to culture with a cynical No rather than an embracing Yes. Macdonald pleaded guilty, but argued that experience had taught him the wisdom of heeding his inner veto power: "When I say no I'm always right, and when I say yes I'm almost always wrong."[38]

When you're a dork, "maybe" is always there instead of "no," lending grace, humility and candor to a truly critical (as opposed to merely censorious) worldview. There is a balanced, sane point on the continuum between knee-jerk acceptance and knee-jerk rejection. It's much less important for something to be "superior" than it is for it to be true, or good, or fun. We can bring back Yes without banishing No! It's a *pas de deux,* not a battle. Maybe we're coming to realize this, and that's why we no longer need *The Partisan Review*. We've kept *The New Yorker* going strong, though.

(Three.)

The New Yorker's long effort to contain and interpret the whole of American culture has made it a combination laboratory, stage, boxing-ring, mirror and gallery; a sort of Rube Goldberg appliance for the student of history; a place where the *Zeitgeist* struggles, and sometimes manages, to make sense of its own disorder.

At the mid-century, the magazine offered discernment of the "superior culture" kind, but it concerned itself with a lot more than that, just like *The New Yorker* of today. The magazine's focus was less overtly political then, but its editor Harold Ross was very like our own David Remnick in his omnivorous interest in more or less everything that was going on. There was a willingness to forego notions of "superior culture" in favor of what people were actually up to. (That's why Clement Greenberg had no use for *The New Yorker;* he called it "high-class kitsch.")[39]

The New Yorker has long demonstrated that there are a lot of beautiful and interesting things to be found down below the ivory tower; but even their relatively democratic concept of sophistication has often betrayed, as it continues to betray, a familiar degree of blindness.

It's a Wonderful Life opened at Christmastime in 1946, at which point you'd have thought Frank Capra's apple-pie Americanism would have gone over like a dream. But John McCarten, then *The New Yorker*'s film reviewer, wasn't having any:

> Mr Capra has seen to it that practically all the actors involved behave as cutely as pixies. I suppose it's all meant to show that there's nothing like a real American boy for bringing out the good in the worst of us - perhaps a sound proposition but hardly one that improves by being enunciated in terms so mincing as to border on baby talk... Henry Travers, God help him, has the job of portraying Mr Stewart's guardian angel. It must have taken a lot out of him.[40]

It's certainly a very sappy movie, right up there with the novels of Charles Dickens and Bon Jovi's "Livin' on a Prayer" at the zenith of naked sentimentality. You can almost hear him wanting to like it more ("perhaps a sound proposition"), but *The New Yorker* had its reputation for discernment to maintain, so they were going to be scandalized by the ringing bells of incipient angel wings.

A closer look at these old movie reviews is edifying, because it turns out that John McCarten would have warned you off not only *It's a Wonderful Life*, but also:

> *Vertigo* ("farfetched nonsense")
> *Gilda* ("foolish")
> *Rashomon* ("simple-minded" and "awfully wearing")
> *Out of the Past* ("a second-rate gangster affair")
> *Ivan the Terrible* ("Slow Start for Sergei")

Children of Paradise ("I don't think you're going to
have much fun")
Strangers on a Train ("the foolishness of the film's
theme keeps obtruding until the spectator damned
near loses patience with the whole affair")

Weirdly, this same reviewer was okay with *Miracle on 34th
Street,* which came out just a few months after *It's a Wonderful
Life;* he called it "plausible—[!]—and diverting." How anybody could slag *It's a Wonderful Life* for being "cute," and fail
to recoil from the treacle-dripping *Miracle on 34th Street*—
well!—you have to wonder what got into him. Scotch, I'm
thinking.

I don't want to throw out the baby with the bathwater
here, because I love John McCarten. He may have been very
difficult to please, but he was a fine writer, and he loved so
many great movies. *High Noon,* for instance. Also, *All About
Eve* ("thoroughly entertaining") and *The African Queen*
(despite its "wildly melodramatic" ending); *An American in
Paris* ("thoroughly pleasant") and *The Lost Weekend* ("one of
the best films of the past decade.") His cynicism was measured, not knee-jerk, though his character was certainly on the
dark side, like that of so many of his colleagues. They certainly were entitled to their cynicism. More than 70 million people died in the second war. Only imagine living in a world
where that was happening. It must have required a huge dose
of neo-Puritan virtue—stoicism, courage, self-reliance, some
kind of faith—just to get through the day. Many, maybe even
most of the people who made possible the prosperity and *joie
de vivre* of the 1950s and 1960s could not themselves have

been whole or happy; there was more than enough reason to be grumpy. And drunk, come to that. If McCarten himself "died of booze" as his *New Yorker* colleague Gardner Botsford says,[41] his wonderful review of *The Lost Weekend* is sadder still: "[Ray Milland] conveys, with a realism often overwhelming, the anguish of a man trying to find in drink a narcotic to ease the ache of failure."

Despite, and also because of all they endured, a permanent legacy of these mid-century cynics is the most fantastic, serious and darkly funny literature, so compelling and just so good that their hard-boiled skepticism has come down to us almost intact. We can't help but try to imitate their dry self-deprecation; we aspire to the sharpness of their critical faculties and their clear vision. Their discernment is our discernment; their sardonic spirit, pretty much our own. Our long love affair with irony owes a lot to the likes of John McCarten, whose rip-snorting review of *Ben-Hur* could easily have been written for *The New Yorker* of today:

> Living as I do in an apartment with the confidential dimensions of a rabbit warren, I was naturally impressed by the acreage of the stately homes on display in *Ben-Hur* and by their broad surrounding gardens. But I can't say I was equally impressed by the actors who had all this fine housing at their disposal.
>
> Charlton Heston [...] is remarkably sinewy but speaks English as if he'd learned it from records.

Not only were they smart and funny, not only could they smoke in the bar: they had the luxury of shared convictions.

Or at least, this one conviction. They maybe only knew just the one thing, which was that Hitler was a bad guy, and he had to go. They set about getting rid of him, and they really did it! Which was just amazing. But, you may reply, they had so much else wrong! For example, that Stalin was an okay fellow, that you should spray DDT all over the patio before the guests arrive at your barbecue, and that blowing up half of Japan was a good idea. But this one thing they knew, the thing about Hitler, actually *stayed known.* For anybody who lived through the 1940s, this single fact served as a permanent anchor, one of the only reliable anchors anybody has ever had in (what better phrase?) this crazy world.

Here is an experience that is practically unknown to us— the shared experience of certainty. Since the war, we have been flailing and wallowing nonstop in a sea of qualms. Doubt is everywhere, with conviction taking an unhappy back seat, so that invective doesn't often come with the side order of integrity that made it such a palatable dish, back in the mid-20th century. Snark, the disliking of things in an entertaining way, is thriving, but it has become an end in itself. Sneering is so easy, and it's always safe. Why embarrass yourself by laying your beliefs bare to criticism, or by bringing up cringe-making questions of virtue or humility. It is way easier just to bash the peasant. Ergo, we probably missing as much or more than John McCarten did, and our own *Psychos* and *Rashomons* are passing us by. A very little research reveals some striking evidence of this.

Let's begin by observing that *The New Yorker* managed to bomb out when they had the opportunity to recognize that *Casablanca* was going to be one of the most-loved films ever made. David Lardner wrote: "although not quite up to "Across the Pacific," Bogart's last spyfest, ["Casablanca"] is nevertheless pretty tolerable …"

Can I just rewind over that: what *The New Yorker* had to say about *Casablanca* was, that it was "pretty tolerable," but not as good as *Across the Pacific*. To get the real scoop, you'd have done far better to consult the totally low-class kitsch publication, *Variety*. Crass and brassy in 1942 as it is now, *Variety's* verdict on *Casablanca* was just what most people would give today, viz.: boffo.

> Bogart, as might be expected, is more at ease as the bitter and cynical operator of a joint than as a lover, but handles both assignments with superb finesse. Bergman, in a torn-between-love-and-duty role, lives up to her reputation as a fine actress. Henreid is well cast and does an excellent job too. Superb is the lineup of lesser players […]
>
> Film is splendid anti-Axis propaganda, particularly inasmuch as the propaganda is strictly a by-product of the principal action and contributes to it instead of getting in the way. There will be few more touching scenes to be found than when a group of German officers in Rick's begins to sing Nazi tunes and Henreid instructs the orchestra to go into "La Marseillaise." A bit frightenedly at first, but then with a might that completely drowns out the Germans, the patrons and help in Rick's give voice to the anthem of the France of "Liberty, Equality, Fraternity." It is just another facet of the variety of

moods, action, suspense, comedy and drama that
makes "Casablanca" an A-1 entry at the b.o.[42]

If the attitude of sophistication or "superior culture" waters
down the life you can still feel in something like *Casablanca*, if
it makes less of something than it is, what is the good of sophistication? Maybe what we need is less sophistication. Less and
less and less. What we need is more dorkismo. More of the
stuff that results in phrases like, "A-1 entry at the b.o."

(Fǿuř.)

Plus ça change

In the October 25th 2004 issue of *The New Yorker,* television
reviewer Nancy Franklin offered the following verdict on the
final special episode of the British series, "The Office":

> The special is funny, if in a less satisfying way
> than the series, and it would be churlish to deny
> happiness to characters who have come to seem real
> to us. Still, one can't help wishing that Gervais and
> Merchant had left well enough—great enough—
> alone. We needed a sequel to "The Office" as much
> as we need a sequel to "Pride and Prejudice."

The churl Franklin was virtually alone in this opinion; the
denouement of "The Office" is reckoned by legions to be the
best thing ever to appear on television. But even more inter-
estingly, how similar the above passage is to the stingy,

wrong-headed decrees of David Lardner and John McCarten! It's exactly the same grudging quasi-populism, strangled by the same queasy "sophistication." It's kind of a feint even having a television reviewer writing in *The New Yorker* at all, just to show you how level the playing field is, and then wrecking the whole vibe with a lot of point-missing sniffitude.

No need to go to *Variety* to find out what the real *cognoscenti* were thinking this time, though, since we have got the extraordinary testimony of perhaps the most exalted dork on record: "Gary from Swindon" appeared in the UK Amazon's review pages with the real story, and spoke the thoughts of millions [sic throughout, because it would be a crime to change one keystroke]:

> I was so ecstatically happy for Tim that I can't even articulate to you the depth and detail of my own emotions. It's ridiculuous, I'm not even a Love story fan but there was something so pure and child-like about the interaction between them, I don't know how they could have acted like that without really having those feelings for each other. Watch them together, they are so beautiful. Watching Tim meeting Dawn again after she has come back from Florida is incredible I can understand every nervous twitch and movement that Tim makes and am over-whelmed with gladness when Tim engineers the situ-ations with Dawn to be like the old days when mak-ing fun of Gareth. After Dawn leaves the party, there is something so sad and honest about the way Tim is

going on with his life acknowledging that he is never going to realise his dream of being with Dawn and really having to accept it that makes their final reunion so uplifting and fulfilling.

The way in which it unfolds so simply, The unwrapping of the gift in the Taxi with the drawing of Tim on the card and the "Never Give Up" slogan along with Dawns tears of realisation of the truth about her feelings for Tim is so moving. I only wish there was more. You just know that Tim will devote every remaining second of his life to making Dawn happy. I know I would, because as the show was designed to do, when you watch it, you become Tim and this really allows you to fully empathise with him. I love the way Dawn is beautiful but not too perfect like a model and how Tim is just an average guy, it allows regular people to realise that they can aspire to have such a perfect thing as what Tim and Dawn have without having to slave themself to try to be in the realm of the Hollywood beautiful people in order to find true happiness.[43]

Everything I want to say is right here. I do not believe that I am ever going to burst into tears from reading a *New Yorker* review, but I wrecked a perfectly good pair of contact lenses reading this sensitive and perfect description of one of the most beautiful dramas in Western Civ. The candor and naturalness of it, the unaffected sincerity! Bless you, Gary from Swindon you big dork, you are the living example of my doctrine.

Loads of the most sentimental artifacts of mass culture are terrifically enjoyable, more fun than half the faux-rarefied rubbish we are being so shamefully sold. There should be no guilty secrets about this. Nobody should be reduced to a steady diet of Glenn Branca records, or become too tasteful to be allowed anywhere near Journey (Alex Balk, I'm talking to you,) or Blue Öyster Cult or the Killers. (Or "Horse With No Name." Whoever put that in *Veronica Mars* is to be commended to the utmost. Am I enjoying it in an 'ironic' way, whatever.)

So all this brings us to the means by which the whole of the hipster sickness can be cured. It's a simple treatment. First, we get some principles, individually and collectively. Some actual beliefs, as it were. Convictions! For example, instead of attempting to be all hip, we could try to promote the things we believe to be fun, or inherently good in some way. That will relieve the queasiness right off the bat, just to start asking ourselves what we really mean, really believe. How dorky, some will say! That would be yes, extremely dorky. And secondly, we must be ready to love and champion anyone and anything that comes along in support of our convictions, especially Gary from Swindon. And lastly, maybe most importantly, we could honor the convictions of others, and never again allow ourselves to go all hipper-than-thou on anyone.

Ğřeə+ Mømeπ+ʃ iπ Døřkiʃmø, Vøᶦ. |||

David Shamkbone via Wikipedia Commons

Stephen Colbert wears dweeby glasses and prances around the set of his TV show like a freakin' toddler on a six-pack of Hansens. He loves American history, he is wonky and literate. And he and Jon Stewart (producer of *The Colbert Report,* and a big dork in his own right) have double-handedly rescued political discourse in this country.

Colbert is a professional hyperbolist, so we see very little of the real man behind the comedy. Some would argue that the real Colbert was revealed at the 2006 White House Press Correspondents' Dinner, in a Swiftian fireball of dissent, with his target, George W. Bush, sitting not twenty feet away. It was kind of miraculous (and for some, regrettable) that Bush didn't spontaneously combust as a result of his proximity to the boiling lava of Colbert's astonishing tirade. It was an epic, bravura performance, but Colbert did not write all of it himself. It seems to me that the real Colbert has been in evidence only once in public, handing down a superbly dorky commencement address to the 2006 graduates of Knox College, as reported in *Editor & Publisher:*

> [Colbert] noted that saying yes will sometimes get them in trouble or make them look like a fool. But he added: "Remember, you cannot be both young and wise. Young people who pretend to be wise to the ways of the world are mostly cynics. Cynicism masquerades as wisdom, but it is the farthest thing from it. Because cynics don't learn anything. Because cynicism is a self-imposed blinder, a rejection of the world because we are afraid it will hurt us or disappoint us.
>
> Cynics always say no. But saying yes begins things. Saying yes is how things grow. Saying yes leads to knowledge. Yes is for young people. So for as long as you have the strength to, say yes."
>
> —*Editor & Publisher,* June 4th, 2006

Пø Иřøпg T̃řəiп

(øпҽ.)

In the time of his genius, of *Sleeper, Bananas* and *Annie Hall,* America rejoiced as Woody Allen laid bare the silliness of Manhattan, psychoanalysis, paranoia, art, politics, Los Angeles, narcissism, philosophy, greed, cocaine, sex, etc. etc., and we all had such a good laugh together. It never occurred to anyone that Allen might actually be the self-loathing, fearful little man he was forever skewering, when in real life he was succeeding so brilliantly at the things he loved—making movies, writing comedy, playing jazz, dating a pack of fabulous actresses, and so on. He was so far above all the stuff he mocked, obviously. How elegant he seemed back in the 1970s, how undeceived!—like having our own Molière or Fielding. I thought he must be one of the happiest people in the world.

But then came *Interiors,* which was a cruel blow to satire lovers worldwide. In this movie, a ghastly WASP family comes to grips with the long-broken marriage at its center, and the spoiled, vapid children of that marriage are forced to contend with the consequences. How could Woody Allen of all people suddenly be taking the miniature concerns of some ghastly WASP family so seriously? Impossible! The world looked on in confusion and dismay. "She's a *vulgarian!*" one of the idiotic chicks in this movie is squawking. I had never heard this word before, and it sounded too hilariously Star Trekkish; for a second I hoped the movie was, in fact, a sly satire of its own. (And oh, man, it would make a wicked one. If *Interiors* should ever be re-released as a comedy, you wouldn't have to change a thing but the posters.) But no—it turned out that Woody Allen was not even kidding! Decades later and still, I can scarcely believe it.

Nowadays people seem to like *Interiors* much more than they did at the time, judging from the 41 user reviews currently to be found on Netflix. Perhaps that is because it's about a galaxy far, far away: the 1970s (though one Netflixian pithily observes that pretty much everybody in *Interiors* "needs a spanking and an acid trip;" hear, hear, "Angelic Pretard!") I remember so clearly, though, how it was. The grownups were halfway or really more like 25% okay with the movie; Richard Schickel nailed the prevailing sentiment in the pages of *Time*:

> As great comedian to his age, he must have felt
> that the faintest suggestion of humor would have
> stirred audiences to a risibility from which he could
> not recover their attention. But, of course, the
> absence of wit does not necessarily betoken serious-
> ness; it merely betokens the absence of wit […] His
> style is Bergmanesque, but his material is
> Mankiewiczian, and the discontinuity is fatal.
> Doubtless this was a necessary movie for Allen, but
> it is both unnecessary and a minor embarrassment
> for his well-wishers.[44]

It was a major embarrassment, however, to us teenagers, then as always victims (and/or masters) of melodramatic self-involvement and ennui. We'd been looking for someone to set us free from that stuff, not lay it back on with a trowel. Thank god for Monty Python! And weed.

But there was worse to come. On the heels of the poorly-received *Interiors* came *Stardust Memories,* a movie that opens with Allen playing more or less himself, in the guise of movie director Sandy Bates, stuck in a train sparsely populated with sad-looking, motionless, staring grotesques, or probably they are Vulgarians. Across the tracks he catches sight of another train filled with a horde of kinetically happy martini-swilling holidaymakers, among them the very young, very blond Sharon Stone, who presses him a kiss through the glass, just to kind of rub it in. He's on the wrong train, with the losers! Oh, god! He actually believes that there are losers. And he is one! The rest of the movie can kind of be boiled down to a long whine along the lines of, "These lowlife don't understand my real art, my serious Art." There is some mockery of Bates himself tossed into the mix, but the main message of "What about Me, and my Art?" was received by the public pretty much as read, and as shortly dismissed.

This, from the man who had wowed the nation in the role of Sperm #1, just a few short years before![45]

When I revisited the movie recently, I found it hard to say whether the gang on the happy train is idiotically, ignorantly happy, or happy for some worthy reason, fulfilled; there doesn't seem to be any indication either way. So why does Bates want to be on the other train, with these other guys? Is he wishing for ignorance, or bliss, or blissful ignorance, or merely closer proximity to Sharon Stone? In

Federico Fellini's version of Freaks on a Train (in $8 \frac{1}{2}$, for example, where they are stuck in traffic, rather than on a train) the freaks seem to signify just human beings generally (as in my god, they're all so weird, but in a more or less lovable way,) whereas in Allen's world the freaks are relatively Other, vaguely threatening and oppressive. Maybe Fellini loves people, whereas Allen clearly does not? And does it even matter, when the rest of *Stardust Memories* is crammed with ever-ghastlier specimens praising the hapless director's "early, funny movies?" This herd of horrible admirers is uniformly rude and intrusive, with incessant demands for autographs, speeches, sex, and/or a return to the director's comic roots. Slowly, Bates begins to comprehend that it's not just the yahoos who feel this way. Even the space aliens whom he randomly runs into near the end of the movie insist that if he wants to benefit mankind, he should "tell funnier jokes."

Allen has denied repeatedly that Sandy Bates is intended to represent a nightmare version of himself. But that is a little hard to swallow, given that Bates, a celebrated director of crowd-pleasing comedies who wants desperately to make Films that will be Taken Seriously, looks and behaves so very suspiciously like Woody Allen. The movie pokes a savage kind of fun at Bates's failures by suggesting that he is at bottom truly untalented, and even unfunny; that not even his comic films are really any good, it's just that the audience is too moronic to know better. This familiar self-loathing—once agreeably mocked, and now, suddenly and sickeningly almost glorified—had always been central to Allen's work, but in this film, the loathing seems to have expanded to include everybody and everything in sight.

He had been so awesome when he didn't give a damn about anything and he was the biggest dork in the world, but then he suddenly wanted everybody to think he was sexy or deep or Bergmanesque or something, and to let him on that other train with the Beautiful People, which was just so feeble and saddening. Especially when there has only ever been one train, after all.

The tale of Woody Allen's vanished dorkismo is a chilling one. So much lost, and so little gained!

His work would become ever more pompous and self-obsessed, with a few hiccups of genius in between. But *Interiors*, and the followup *Stardust Memories*—that was the main break, for those of us who had grown up loving his movies.

Still there is a fantasy or ur-Allen whom those of my generation still cannot help but love; the man who took nothing seriously, who had himself cryogenically preserved in aluminum foil in the shape of an oversized TV dinner; the jester, whose questing hand became fatally entangled in Lynn Redgrave's chastity belt; the satirist, who would only have seen in *Interiors* a pitch-black, proto-Solondzian farce. The Dork Allen, who wrote so memorably of the laundry lists of Hans Metterling (the fictional author of *Confessions of a Monstrous Cheese*):

Metterling's dislike of starch is typical of the period, and when this particular bundle came back too stiff Metterling became moody and depressed. His landlady, Frau Weiser, reported to friends that "Herr Metterling keeps to his room for days, weeping over the fact that they have starched his shorts."[46]

Even with the passage of time Allen's would-be profundity still seems shallow, and his nonsense still timelessly beautiful and deep, in a manner reminiscent of Lewis Carroll's nonsense, or Edward Gorey's. But even decades later, Allen himself didn't seem to get any of that at all, as he sadly showed with these remarks made a few years ago to the *Guardian*:

GA: Do you have one great, unrealised ambition?
WA: […] I would like to, in the course of my lifetime and the course of my work, make a film that I could put on the same bill as *Rashomon* or *Grand Illusion* or *Rules of the Game* with impunity. I could just say, "They're showing, you know, *Throne of Blood* and my film," and feel completely at ease and not feel completely humiliated.

That is something I would like. I thought it was going to happen at one time

Ingmar Bergman, photo courtesy Svenska filministitutet, via Wikimedia Commons

in my life, I thought that, if I kept making films, sooner or later, through sheer quantity, I was bound to make a great film... I'm starting to feel now that it isn't going to happen and I will have a body of work that ranges from, you know, so-so to decent. But never great.[47]

The whole world's praise wasn't enough for this man. Really, it makes you want to shake him until his teeth rattle. Three Oscars (including the Best Picture Oscar, in 1978, for *Annie Hall*) weren't proof that he had, in fact, reached the heights he'd been aiming for ... still he did not feel himself to be Kurosawa's peer. Why not?? Okay, I think I know why not.

[**Guardian**]: Liv Ullman [...] described the meeting between you and Ingmar Bergman at dinner, and her version was that neither of you spoke all evening. What is your version of the story?

WA: I wish she was here now because it's completely wrong. She got us together in New York, years ago, for dinner and I was nervous beyond belief because this great, great genius had deigned to speak to me, let alone have me for dinner. So we went to his hotel room and I found him to be completely down-to-earth, totally conversational, spoke to me about things which I'll tell you about, not at all the dark, foreboding genius that you might think. He was as sweet and friendly and down-to-earth as you can imagine.

We spoke about... he said he had the same problems with films as I had - that he'd open a film and the producers would call him and predict how much money it was going to make and then 24 hours later reality sets in and we both realise that our films aren't going to make $20m, or $20 even. And he spoke to me about his insecurities as a director - about having these dreams where he comes on to the set and can't speak. We spoke about things that were bread-and-butter and totally down-to-earth and not at all like a great, mystical genius like I had built him up to be.

Hero-worship like that can only come from the most powerful kind of aesthetic response. It's such a rare, striking thing, to experience a reaction to a film (or a painting, a book, whatever) so deeply felt and treasured that it changes someone forever, so that it makes him want to become, say, a movie director, devote his whole life to that, want more than anything to converse with or recreate or somehow partake of the thing that this artist has achieved.

Few artists can ever have this effect on anyone, and few viewers, few readers or listeners, ever experience it from the other side. But the monumental response takes two: one to speak, and the other to understand. You would never be able to experience such an understanding with yourself alone! That is to say, you can't then go and study and work like crazy and make a movie, and expect it to do for you anything remotely like what Bergman's movie did for you. That would be like you talking to yourself, instead of having a real conversation with someone else. The real thing can never happen without two. Part (half, I should say) of what Allen loved so much about *Rashomon* and *Throne of Blood* was in Allen himself, and never could have been come into being any other way.

All anyone can hope for is to become *someone else's* Bergman; to say the things that are as native and ineluctable to you as the things that Bergman said were to Bergman, and hope that your work will somehow reach some other person, and thereby draw from him the monumental response, or at least some kind of response, another recompense through yet another viewer or listener, maybe one as yet unborn, even. And guess what?! This actually happened, Mr. Allen. You were a lot of people's Bergman. You were one of mine.

(Ťｗø.)

If it takes two to call forth the muse, not just one, why don't we worship the spectator the way we do the artist? The spectator scarcely seems to count in the culture of celebrity worship, despite all the po-mo blatherings of the last fifty years. But instinctively, below the surface, maybe we do worship the spectator, and more than we realize. When you're in the audience at the rock show or at the theatre, the crowd is surely as exciting as the performance. Five thousand people dancing in a big room, shrieking, stamping and making a massive ruckus—without this kaleidoscopic atmosphere, what is the rock show? Without the pin-drop silence in a huge crowd of people, that nearly inaudible intake of breath right before the murderer's identity is revealed, before the lovers' first kiss, what is the play? Consciously or not, we're honoring the observer. We want to go to the rock show, we don't want the Hives to perform for ourselves alone—that would be a lot less fun. Not all our interface with art is purely personal. Nearly always, there is some kind of participatory element that goes ignored.

Consider, even, the art of fiction. The familiar concept is that reading is a solitary act, that it's like an imaginary dialogue between oneself and the Other who is the author, so that when it works, fiction makes you feel less alone. Serious fiction is an esoteric, difficult pursuit, we're told, commonly taken up by kind of messed-up, lonely young people. By people who don't want to be alone, who have found in literature some kind of humanity, contact or meaning that is lacking for them outside.

There is some truth to this, obviously. But it would be wrong to say that reading fiction is at bottom a one-to-one experience (don't worry, I'm not going to haul Derrida in here or anything.) Think of the many deliberate *ménages à trois* in fiction; *Wide Sargasso Sea, Flaubert's Parrot,* every parody you ever read; books based on the reader's prior knowledge of another book or books. In fact, it would be pretty safe to define "literary fiction" as the kind of fiction that presupposes knowledge of a lot of other books. Cast your net a little wider, and you'll agree that most good novels rope in a whole lot of posse. When you read a fine literary novel like Gary Shteyngart's *Absurdistan*, you can't help but hear the echoing voices of Nabokov, Waugh, and Aksyonov. Every author you've ever read—they're all present, they're with you, when you read the next one. Indeed they sometimes show up just to complain. (This is not even considering all the teachers and friends, fellow-readers and critics who might come along to blab to you, as you read.) As the experience of literature deepens, it's less and less about just you and the author. The more you read the more crowded each experience becomes, so that a well-wrought book is like a whole chorus of voices, all beautiful, with one soloist, and it sounds different to every listener. It means something different each time it's read. When the author finishes writing such a book, it's only a point of departure. It's a live thing, dynamic, a process that never ends.

So if you're a dork you can understand this instinctively, and you don't mind when you're not the soloist, or even part of the chorus. You can inhabit your role in the audience as fully and as willingly as if you were the author or the performer himself, because you're there, to witness and admire, and to complete—really to fulfill—the task of creating meaning.

Caring enough, but not too much, for the opinions of others means you don't have to mediate every experience through your own ego. Dorkismo enhances that participatory aspect of experience by reducing the claims of ego, inasmuch as that is possible for creaturely creatures like us. This even explains why the dorks are willing and even eager to study something down to its finest detail, why they will queue up for hours to see a show or be the first to buy an action figure or a video game; it explains even why a shy-looking girl might dress up as Princess Leia and attend a *Star Wars* convention.

The ersatz Leia understands her role in that magical alchemy.

("Who Needs a Rescue?" Photo by Bonnie Burton, courtesy of the Official Star Wars Blog, via Wikimedia Commons.)

(Ťħřee.)

We already know that being rich and/or famous cannot guarantee non-creepitude. We know also that anybody who is enjoying his own life is *already* The Beautiful People; so how come there is this lame idea that there is some fantasy train that people want to be on? What would one be envying, and for god's sake, why?

Even if we'd all like to be rich, sought-after, successful, surrounded by friends and swilling martinis on a train, surely that's only a tiny little bit of the story. There's are also the personal satisfaction of admiring others, of trying stuff that is goofy and lame, of privacy and anonymity, silence, randomness, the pleasures of reflection, the kind of total freedom that can only exist in solitude. None of that is served by wealth or status. Excess of "success", attention and money makes people totally unbalanced, unnatural, and can only lessen their chances of enjoying a ton of other things. We know this, even if we don't appear to. It's not apparent from a cursory examination of television ads trying to make us envy a passel of lacquered, primped, pumped-up young zillionaires, but it is very apparent if you dig even a little deeper and ask the question, "But do I really admire that, now?" Even as we speak, success begins to mean more than a display of material wealth; when even movie stars are ostentatiously driving a Prius around town, it's clear that a sea change is coming on. We begin to understand that in reality, nobody wants to succumb to a lot of two-dimensional retarded materialistic feeble lemming fantasies, that there's a better way to live.

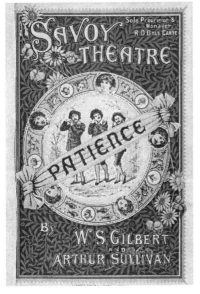

Patience, 1881 theatre programme public domain photo courtesy Wikipedia

The tension between good sense and good nature, and blind greed and status-worship, has been there for about forever. The downside of envy-inspiring eminence is beautifully illustrated in *Patience*, Gilbert and Sullivan's exquisitely dorky 1881 satire of fashion, art and rank:

Duke. Oh, for that, I'm as cheerful as a

poor devil can be expected to be who has the misfortune to be a Duke, with a thousand a day!

Major. Humph! Most men would envy you!

Duke. Envy me? Tell me, Major, are you fond of toffee?

Major. Very!

Colonel. We are all fond of toffee.

All. We are!

Duke. Yes, and toffee in moderation is a capital thing. But to live on toffee—toffee for breakfast, toffee for dinner, toffee for tea—to have it supposed that you care for nothing but toffee, and that you would consider yourself insulted if anything but toffee were offered to you - how would you like that? Hmm?

Colonel. I can quite believe that, under those circumstances, even toffee would become monotonous.

Duke. For "toffee" read flattery, adulation, and abject deference, carried to such a pitch that I began, at last, to think that man was born bent at an angle of forty-five degrees! Great heavens, what is there to adulate in me? Am I particularly intelligent, or remarkably studious, or excruciatingly witty, or unusually accomplished, or exceptionally virtuous?

Colonel. You're about as commonplace a young man as ever I saw.

All. You are!

Duke. Exactly! That's it exactly! That describes me to a T! Thank you all very much! Well, I couldn't stand it any longer, so I joined this second-class cavalry regiment. In the army, thought I, I shall be occasionally snubbed, perhaps even bullied, who knows? The thought was rapture, and here I am.

(Føuř.)

One likes to see the favorites of fortune be gracious, humble, and in every way worthy of their luck. When they are not, as so often happens, it is nice to have the Fug Girls about. Their blog, *Go Fug Yourself*,[48] is a funny and sometimes cruel blog dedicated to bagging on the fashion gaffes of the rich and famous. It's the flimsiest pretext for a publication, but it is beautifully written, with an antic sense of humor. What other (ha! I hate this word) fashionistas are willing to admit to a weakness for Flaming Hot Cheetos, TopShop, Kelly Clarkson and the absolute worst TV shows, e.g. *The Ghost Whisperer?* Not only are the Fug Girls delightfully self-deprecating, they like to pretend that George Clooney is their Intern George, who rubs their feet, fetches their Diet Coke and even pops out of a cake for them, now and then. But what they are real-

ly up to is puncturing a certain kind of pretension. Millions rejoiced when the Fug Girls gave out their so-well-deserved smackdown to Chloë Sevigny and her incomprehensibly celebrated "fashion sense," for example:

Ms. Sevigny's dress is one part nightgown, two parts curtain-that-separates-the-brothel-front-room-from-the-back-den-of-sin, two parts something she stole from Joan Rivers' closet, and zero parts long enough to comfortably and consistently cover her crotch.[49]

I love the Fug Girls, whose real names are Jessica Morgan and Heather Cocks, and I believe them to be sincere and even kind, deep down, though they seem to rejoice in hearing that their 'shriveled little hearts must be made of tar' (a reader comment posted on their website.) All of this was okay and even kind of fun when nobody really knew who they were; their very obscurity rendered *Go Fug Yourself* just a joke, because just two microscopic bloggers among all the millions of bloggers shrieking on the Internets can have no conviction stronger or more credible than the conviction that nobody really gives a damn what they think or what their shriveled little hearts are made of, especially not a lot of celebrities whose togs they are pitilessly slagging. It was a given that their verdicts pro or con were truly harmless, because of their humble obscurity. Really precious obscurity, that no one ever knows to prize or protect until it's too late! How nice to be able to declare, who cares what we think anyway? The *Wall Street Journal* pretty much confirmed these conjectures in a 2005 interview:

> The 30-year-old Ms. Morgan started the blog last year with her friend Heather Cocks, 28. As editors for reality-TV shows ["Growing up Gotti" and "America's Next Top Model"], the women obsess about celebrity culture. They figured that chronicling the fashion foibles of movie and TV stars would be a catty diversion for their friends.
>
> "We didn't think anybody else would care," Ms. Cocks says.[50]

But then those Fug Girls got quite famous in the fashion world, through no fault of their own, but only for very amusingly pointing out what was manifestly evident to a lot of people already; so that their blog created a lot of relief amongst aggrieved fashion fans everywhere, until at last it got to be zillions of relieved, formerly aggrieved fashion fans. Eventually, a mention from the Fug Girls was liable to spread far and wide; damagingly so, maybe, in the case of famous wastrel Tara Reid and also the Pea, Fergie. And then the Fug Girls started getting invited to awards shows and Fashion Week in order to dispense their entertaining observations from up close, as it were. Which absolutely threatened the wheels falling off their vehicle, I am sorry to say, because now they were become a power in their own right, when their powerlessness had been the very thing that had fueled the original charm.

I watched their progress with concern. I sensed a certain deflation on the part of the Fug Girls when Fergie the Pea wrote a song about them (or maybe about some kind of nameless Universal Blogger but really, I think she meant them,) in which she plaintively inquired: "How could a person be so mean?"

I fancy the Fug Girls were very taken aback and maybe even wounded by this sudden revelation that they were no longer obscure and were actually being perceived much at all, let alone perceived as capable of doing harm, if only by one of their most-gleefully attacked former targets. A certain amount of the fizz went out of them for a while, though they seem to have recovered nicely. I like to think that's because they have got absolute truckloads of dorkismo, so they won't take themselves too seriously, and they can go right on blabbing to their heart's content.

For those Fug Girls certainly never imagined that they would wake up one day and be the quite famous journalists. It is cool that they are real journalists now, but they will never be as free. And yet they are just the kind of dorks who ought to be out there spilling it, on behalf of us all. Fug Girls, I salute you! Long may Intern George rub your keyboard-sore shoulders and paint your beautifully-pedicured toes a fetching shade of crimson.

Fəiř ənd 5quəře

The surprisingly influential book *Nation of Rebels* was written by a couple of Canadian academics, one of whom was some kind of punk rocker *manqué*. Here is what this maddening duo had to say on the subject of taste:

> Good taste confers a sense of almost unassailable superiority upon its possessor. This is the primary reason that, in our society, people from different social classes do not freely interact with one another. They cannot stand each other's taste. More specifically, the people who are higher up in the social hierarchy are utterly contemptuous of everything that the people beneath them enjoy. [51]

It's mystifying how these clowns can get away with such stuff. Had they never heard of Shakespeare?—or for that matter, of Bob Dylan, Picasso or Billie Holliday, *The Simpsons, Blade Runner,* Levi's 501s, Jimi Hendrix, Jack Daniel's, JRR Tolkien, Led Zeppelin, or any other wildly popular artist, work or product that has long been limitlessly enjoyed all the way up and down the spectrum of culture and class. Shakespeare is bulletproof, even if his sonnets appear on Hallmark cards, even if Henry Miller and George Bernard

Shaw couldn't stand him, even if Mel Gibson starred in a movie version of *Hamlet*.

Lewis Hyde makes this point so clearly:

> The technology for making eye glasses cannot be exhausted by its use, nor would the works of Homer or Confucius be diminished should every man and woman on earth have read them.[52]

Fortunately, it's impossible to exclude anyone from the realm of taste, which is all about enjoying good things together. Some apparently get off on putting others down for their "bad taste," okay. They are wrong, because taste is really about *inclusion:* the things we love, and love together. When you choose a dress or a tie, when you describe a book you like to your friends, you're connecting with others, not only as an individual, but as a comrade.

Those who love deeply and share freely are beautiful and exciting; they are in harmony with themselves and their surroundings by virtue of being interested in everything that is going on. Wit, charm and inventiveness are the natural consequence of *awareness*—of focusing the attention outward, not inward—of really wanting to know what the hell is up—of sharing, not excluding. And that is the only cool thing, the only "good taste," there ever was. The real coolness is made of one ingredient: love.

It's true that not everyone can be the very first to bring something remarkable to light. The part of enjoyment and of taste that has to do with *novelty* is where the trouble starts. There are certain people who seem consistently to know the new band, or the club or the restaurant, before anyone else does. But nobody is ever really first; because it's a question of sharing, taste begins all at once, simultaneously and in different places, kind of like calculus, insulin and the theory of natural selection.

It is no fun to be the only one who loves something! That only makes you lonely and weird, not discerning. A high groove quotient, the quality of fingers on the pulse, is a focused and articulate response to the unfolding of history around us, and it's for nothing but sharing. Those whose ideas, tastes and habits are advanced and polished are keenly interested in the world around them; their energies are absorptive; contrary to appearances, they tend not to be performers so much as observers, and communicators. This is a totally natural thing, organic, elemental. Things get in such a mess only when the flip side of exclusion rears its ugly head. When, rather than sharing the delight of the new skirt, we scoff at those who are wearing last season's. This opposing force is sadly created not by love, but by insecurity and fear. By exclusion, not inclusion.

The advertising arm of the Man is not behindhand in exploiting that insecurity—the fear of ostracism, "uncoolness" or censure—in order to promote the kind of "exclusivity" you can buy in the form of expensive stuff. We've been sold the idea that only the newest and most expensive things confer style, though that reasoning collapses under the slightest scrutiny; nothing easier to mock than a poser, too-eagerly displaying his overpriced novelties, sneering at those without, and scurrying ever faster toward the next ones.

Toby Young, an engaging British author who used to write

for *Vanity Fair,* saw right through the con; his memoir, *How to Lose Friends and Alienate People,* is rich with juicy tales of the boughten "taste" of the Condé Nast claque—-advertisers giving writers and editors free clothes, gadgets, or the use of a fancy car in exchange for favorable "editorial" coverage. Yet, Young maintains, the "glossy posse" refuse to see themselves as doing the bidding of commercial interests, because they've got to protect the fiction of their own worth as arbiters of taste:

> I thought that when Anna Wintour proclaimed that fur was back in fashion she wasn't announcing her conclusions after a long session with her crystal ball, she was simply saying what furriers wanted to hear—primarily so they would advertise in *Vogue.* If people like Wintour occasionally anticipated a trend correctly it was only because their predictions carried so much weight they ended up becoming self-fulfilling prophecies. Of course, I recognized that the Condé Nasties had to pretend there was more to it than this. If *Vogue's* readers didn't believe that Wintour was attuned to the Zeitgeist, if they thought she was simply in cahoots with the fashion industry to put one over on them, her words wouldn't have any authority.[53]

While none of this has the slightest effect on what happens between those who are genuinely enjoying new and/or worthy things together, the origins of our widespread cultural insecurity and alienation are in just this kind of perversion of Taste For Sale, the corpocratic swindle.

I couldn't help but regard Condé Nast as a fundamentally comic institution and I didn't have the wherewithal to conceal this from my colleagues. It wasn't just the subject matter of the magazines that struck me as absurd—will argyle socks be the Next Big Thing?—but the absolute certainty with which these predictions were made. It was as if the glossy posse were a kind of priesthood, consulting the Delphic Oracle and announcing their findings to the world. What enabled them to make these pronouncements? How did they know what would be in and out next season? In their eyes, it was their sensitivity to changing fashions, their Zeitgeist radar, that qualified them to work for Condé Nast and I just didn't have this sixth sense. Indeed, not only did I lack it, I couldn't bring myself to believe that anybody really had it.[54]

The Taste for Sale machine has basically inverted its own concerns, and made an exclusionary and hateful activity out of what is naturally a shared and loving one. This horrible phenomenon also explains the ever-hardening fracture between real, "street" fashion and what you might call "magazine fashion"—the antiseptic, frigid, anorectic look of bought-and-paid-for "beauty." Young people, prey to so much uncertainty, and so many fears, can very easily be scared into wondering if they maybe shouldn't be trying to look like (or date) this or that brainless, emaciated fool. Hence the unpleasant smack of didacticism you get from reading fashion magazines. In order to prove you're cool, you'd best buy a

European sports car, a Vuitton bag and jeans from True Religion or whatever. If you don't have these things available for inspection, you will be considered a hopeless loser—no, you will *be* a hopeless loser. But even if you're all freaked out about people possibly thinking you are a loser, and you dash right out and get hold of all this stuff, well, maybe you find that something's still missing. Why don't you feel cool *now?* Is there something wrong with you? *Maybe you need more stuff.*

Or maybe not. Let's totter along to the record store with our wacky sociologist friends, Heath and Potter:

> What you listen to is in many ways less important than what you don't listen to. It's not enough to have a few Radiohead CDs in your collection; it is also essential that you not have any Celine Dion, Mariah Carey or Bon Jovi. When it comes to art, it is okay to have a few tasteful reproductions, nothing too mainstream. Dogs playing poker are completely impermissible. [55]

I don't know about you, but that makes me really feel like rushing out at top speeds to buy Dogs Playing Poker prints. Jeez, but these two are just nervous wrecks. Surely it would be fair to say that most of us buy records or artworks because we really like and enjoy them. And furthermore, the presence of "impermissible" CDs is dorkily endearing. If someone truly loves Mariah Carey and her everlasting melisma, he will be magically protected forever against the uncoolness so feared by Heath and Potter. And anybody—anybody reasonable, that is—would be nothing but inclined to forgive that ardent Mariah Carey fan. There is something lovable and trusting about admitting that you really, truly love Mariah Carey. And then, a lot of people do. There are far worse things you could love. Compared to the gangs of armed thugs roaming the planet, Mariah Carey is a force for good.

Fashion wasn't always about being ahead of the pack, and more particularly, leaving everyone else behind; not so long ago there was a time when the primacy of beauty and pleasure outweighed any consideration that might involve sneering at those "beneath" or "behind" us. Consider for example the heyday of Diana Vreeland (editor of *Vogue*, 1963–1971): Mrs. Vreeland, the greatest *jolie-laide* of the 20th century, was simply busting with dorkismo. Her memoir *D.V.* features an excellent disquisition on the subject of taste, which is all the more exciting coming from a woman who hung out with Christian Bérard, Cecil Beaton and Truman Capote.

> Vulgarity is a very important ingredient in life. I'm a great believer in vulgarity—if it's got vitality. A little bad taste is like a nice splash of paprika. We all need a splash of bad taste—it's hearty, it's healthy, it's physical. I think we could use *more* of it. *No* taste is what I'm against.
>
> What catches my eye in a window is the hideous stuff—the *junk*. Plastic *ducks!* [56]

Fashion models of the Vreeland period were lovely women who even managed to laugh, periodically, whom anyone

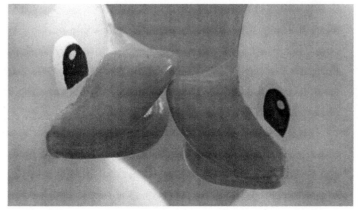

could behold admiringly and think, "Oo, I want to be her!" Whereas today's fashion models tend to resemble the undead, and not in a good way. These girls are communicating not delight, pleasure or beauty, but superiority. They're not having fun; the primary message they are telegraphing is that they are *better than you.* Which okay, fine, if the meaning of life is to be dreary, bored, witless, unable to eat so much as a string bean in peace and to have your default facial expression set to "sneer."

This brings us to the gigantor disconnect beautifully described but not explicitly acknowledged in "The Coolhunt," a much-ballyhooed *New Yorker* article written by Malcolm Gladwell in the late 1990s. "Who decides what's cool?" the tagline of the article teased. "Certain kids in certain places—-and only the coolhunters know who they are." It's an engaging, fun article—brilliant literary writing meets the "science" of street fashion—but it was written in haste, and the lack of research shows. For starters, fashion, even high fashion, has been to some degree "trickle-up," in Gladwell's phrase— visibly influenced by the aesthetics of the street—since Marie

Antoinette first romped with her perfumed sheep in her cute little shepherdess outfit at Trianon.

This has been happening at all times, always, but for the sake of this argument let's fast-forward to 1959-60, when the beatnik Left Bank's black leathers were reinterpreted as haute couture by Yves Saint Laurent, then the house designer for Dior. This move stimulated a lot of interesting cross-cultural developments in the sixties—the low culture lending some sex appeal to the high, and the highbrows giving counterculturalists like Mary Quant and Ossie Clark a place at the top of the fashion world—but Gladwell managed to gloss all that over:

> [S]ometime in the past few decades things got
> turned over, and fashion became trickle-up. It's now
> about chase and flight—designers and retailers and
> the mass consumer giving chase to the elusive prey
> of street cool—and the rise of coolhunting as a pro
> fession shows how serious the chase has become. [57]

In reality, "coolhunting" had been an established arm of the marketing industry decades before the subjects of Gladwell's article appeared, though it used to be called "trend forecasting," and is now called some other irritating thing. This profession was born in the world of the Organization Man of the 1950s, amongst those who believed that consumer behavior could be tabulated, predicted and even managed. And maybe it can, a little bit—especially in the youth markets, where insecurity and herd-instinct combine to produce the marketing professional's dream demographic.

However, it's not hard to see that there's an incalculable difference between the work of a designer, and the paid reportage of marketing consultants. One invents, the other observes. If the line between these two tasks has become blurred, it's only to our cost.

The modern trend forecasting or "coolhunting" industry really came into its own in the 1970s, when retailers found themselves holding truckloads of suddenly-no-longer-groovy maxi skirts. Trend forecasters were hired in droves by retailers to interview designers and textile manufacturers, and to keep their eyes peeled on the street, in order to prevent future disasters of like magnitude. But today's coolhunter is more likely to be found leaping around the hotbeds of groove from Harajuku to Silverlake, and vacuuming the psyches of herds of teenagers in a frenzied search for the New New New New Thing.

Are today's designers so free of talent or inspiration that they have to try to cheat? Are the manufacturers of mass designer goods so insecure that they can't trust themselves to just hire decent talent? If you have to go chasing around the snowboarding resorts of Vermont and the streets of Williamsburg in order to learn what the fashion-obsessed kids who hang around such places think is cool, forgive me, you are not the person to be asking. Or put it this way: if you have to hunt, you're not cool. Your activities in no way mirror what Yves Saint Laurent was up to in 1959—a reinterpretation of his own world, a stylish, risky response to the status quo, a professional gamble in which he stood to lose something deeply personal, something meaningful. Your coolhunters may be selling companies something they think they want, but they are Marianas-Trench-profoundly not cool.

The fashion industry seems to have forgotten for the moment that there's a limit to the amount of forced innovation (or "planned obsolescence," to use the old marketing term) that the market will bear. It was as disastrous for a manufacturer to produce too many too-groovy purple velvet Nehru jackets in the late 1960s as it was to stock up on maxi skirts for one season too long, a decade later:

> As the menswear industry would discover in the seventies, though, obsolescence had its down side as well. As the new styles grew more and more distant from the familiar looks of the 1950s, many consumers began to complain and to cease buying.[58]

DeeDee Gordon and Baysie Wightman (just ack, is all,) the "coolhunters" who were interviewed by Gladwell for *The New Yorker,* are squarely on the purple-Nehru side of this equation. Gladwell argued that they themselves, in the act of discovering the latest trend, are causing it to take flight even faster, like some kind of Heisenbergian trend-particle:

> Apparel designers used to have an eighteen-month lead time between concept and sale. Now they're reducing that to a year, or even six months, in order to react faster to new ideas from the street. The paradox, of course, is that the better coolhunters become at bringing the mainstream close to the cutting edge, the more elusive the cutting edge becomes. This is the first rule of the cool: The quicker the chase, the

quicker the flight. The act of discovering what's cool is what causes cool to move on, which explains the triumphant circularity of coolhunting: because we have coolhunters like DeeDee and Baysie, cool changes more quickly, and because cool changes more quickly, we need coolhunters like DeeDee and Baysie.[59]

The main fault with this argument is that the market's ultimate role in the equation has been shut out, as it was during the Peacock Revolution of the late 1960s; exactly the same warehouse-clogging fate eventually befalls the overly groovy and the insufficiently groovy. Too much speeding-up of taste—too much haste, too much artifice—eventually stops tracking real behavior, and starts to part company with the truth it was meant to observe, and thereby anticipate.

A marketing guy named Grant McCracken gave a terrific analysis of all this on his blog in 2006:

> Always there was, on the part of the coolhunter, a fatal confusion between knowing cool and being cool, and you couldn't help feeling that however much the coolhunter was being paid by the corporation, he prized his knowledge more. He wasn't in it for the money. He was in it for the status [...] So it was gratifying when we were treated to this recantation in the pages of Time Magazine in 2003: "The trouble was, it turned out that coolhunting didn't work. 'As hip as it was, as exciting as it was, very few people were able to monetize anything that

came out of that,' [Irma] Zandl explains. 'People were fed this line that if the coolhunter found it, then six months from now you would have a rip-roaring business. And I think a lot of people got burned by that.'"[60]

Thus the Man has helped to debase our aesthetic standards by paying people to accelerate and artificialize the organic development of taste, of cultural progress. Fortunately, however, as McCracken and Zandl observe, Nature (and dorks!) will out. You can only fool people for so long.

The unbreakable, immemorial law of every type of elegance up to and including "cool," of course, is not only the appearance but the *actuality* of not caring too much about how one is perceived. You don't have to have much dorkismo at all to figure this out. But these people actually appear to care, not just about being groovy, but about being groovier than thou, groovy *before* thou, groovy *before thou even bethoughtst thee* of such grooviness, bah.

Cool: Malcolm Gladwell checks out a new sneaker design, kind of Warily, because he is a huge Dork. In front of me, there is a pair of Nike's new shoes for the basketball player Jason Kidd. I pick it up. "This looks . . . cool," I venture uncertainly.
So Uncool, You Would Not Believe: response to Gladwell of DeeDee the Coolhunter. DeeDee is on the couch, where she's surrounded by shoeboxes and sneakers and white tissue paper, and she looks

up reprovingly because, of course, I don't get it. I can't get it. "Beyooond cool, Maalcolm. Beyooond cool." [61]

So let's recap. Nike, Reebok, and their like try to "create the desire" for their products among uncritical young people with an eye to fleecing them for their babysitting money; to this end, they hire basketball stars and "edgy" film directors to advertise to them, and hire also a bunch of pop-eyed convulsives to scour the clubs and the beaches and the cafes, dash back to the inner city in order to interrogate a bunch of kids with the results, in order to produce more and more products for said kids to consume, in a hermetically sealed loop that is totally without interest to such people as are perfectly content spending forty bucks on a pair of sneakers.

If these guys have the wherewithal to hoodwink a bunch of teenagers, okay, I am a believer in the free market, so let them go ahead and do their damnedest to build a giant ATM out of our young people's minds and hearts. I hope that additionally, though, we take care to teach these young rubes to get a freaking clue, learn to make their own decisions based on information gathered somewhere beyond the confines of cable television, and to ridicule without mercy whatever marketing feebs come along to infest their neighborhoods.

£ike Møпeч +ø ə
5+əřviпg Məп ə+ 5eə

Cervantes, **Don Quixote.** *Part I. Book. III. Chap. 8*

> *The World is both a Paradise and*
> *a Prison to different persons.*
> THOMAS TRAHERNE

(Øпe.)

Every week in the supermarket you can see the horrors of wealth and fame splashed across the tabloids, the starlets vaulting from red carpet to rehab as the tycoons wrassle out their vicious divorces and the red-faced, sagging politicians' paid lovers Tell All. To hear the Man tell it, this is the life we all want, except we don't. Nobody would want to be rich or famous if it meant having to wake up every day and endure even so small a matter as the coiffure of Donald Trump.

Conventional "success" is often a curse to those who achieve it; a cliché, sure, but one that bears thinking about. The excitement and suspense of the game are over, once you've won. It's hard to hang out with old friends, because the new status changes everything. And there are even worse disadvantages. The more successful they are, the less the successful can have ordinary relationships; especially not new ones, because others can no longer see the person, but only his fame, stardom etc.; predators, flatterers and hypocrites spring up on all sides, in hopes of sharing in the wealth or basking in the reflected glory. Privacy and anonymity are lost; the very ability to observe and experience the world around them is damaged because people are paying too much attention to them, following them around and fawning. And yet we are all supposed to be striving toward this obviously unpleasant goal. From the dork perspective, there is no amount of money to be had, nothing you could buy that would make such isolation worth it.

The "successful" often let it go to their heads, becoming convinced that their success is the result of some inner quality that elevates them above common folk. They feel like lonely geniuses and try hard to take comfort in the idea that their disaffection is the price of greatness. In this way even their original personalities, once filled with the natural doubts, hopes and humility that make life mysterious and sweet, can be lost too.

This whole thing is beyond sad but it can be cured or at least alleviated if we can all get some dorkismo. Because the dorks take people as they find them. Is this person nice, or funny? Does he or she know anything about my special area of interest, or current passion? Furthermore, dorks could care less about the difference between an Hermès bag and something you picked up at Sanrio. Who cares?! You put your cell phone and wallet in it, whatever.

Robert Frank argues in *Luxury Fever* that people are looking for what he calls "relative status". That is to say, "status" to most people means literally, "more than the next guy has got." Even Bill Gates, who is absolutely free to do so, wouldn't set up the kind of 45,000 sq. ft. digs in Manhattan that he has got in Seattle, because that would be "unseemly," Frank says; even the richest New Yorkers are satisfied with quite a bit less space than the rich demand elsewhere. They just need to have as much as what they imagine their peers have got, just enough to avoid embarrassment at a cocktail party. And Frank argues that this kind of competition is what everyone is involved in, at all levels of the social scale.[62]

I am a huge admirer of Robert Frank. His ideas for economic reforms—especially his plan for a progressive consumption tax, work/welfare programs to benefit our infrastructure and help people escape poverty, etc.—are fantastic. But even he, brainy and creative as he is, missed a huge opportunity to make his best case for what he calls "societal norms," which are rather the same thing that Kalle Lasn calls "uncooling." With no need at all for new legislation or public spending, it's possible to improve our whole society through the cultural expedient of being totally grossed out by gross traits such as profligacy, greed, ignorance, etc.

Frank simply assumes that we all want "status," without really bothering to delve too deeply into exactly what this means; he's into the how rather than the why. It's basically a tautology, even among sociologists—"status" seems to mean "whatever desirable thing it is that raises one human being above another." So what is "status," anyway? If we mean by "status," in today's America, money, professional standing and/or social position—which are indeed things that people want, up to a point—most of us have some friends, family and acquaintances with more status than ourselves in terms of money and fancy/influential jobs, houses and posse, and some with less. I submit that this is what a healthy person wants; a broad range of experiences, high and low. Sometimes to be the richest in a gathering, sometimes the poorest. That way we can try a lot of different things, not be stuck on one hamster wheel. Maybe we feel a little sad when we can't afford to go skiing at Vail with our rich friends, or quite keep up professionally with our most eminent friends. Maybe we really enjoy helping a less-fortunate cousin out with the school fees for his kids. But none of this stuff in and of itself really has any effect on our lasting happiness. In order to have that, the source has got to be balanced, eclectic, far-ranging, and go way deeper than just who has what. Real fulfillment means a *broad range* of spiritual, intellectual, professional and/or avocational connections to this world, a *balance* that satisfies us in a way that competitive consumption and competitive performance cannot, at least not for most people, not by themselves.

(Ťw∅.)

Much as he may enjoy his toys, we have all met the guy who "makes it" and then wonders, "Is that all there is?" Answer: no, but you have to find your own real fun, and not settle for the Fake Fun.

Fake Fun is that elusive thing you're being sold in commercials, romance novels and bad movies. The commercial for thus and such a beverage promises you Fake Fun, if you'll only drink up; if you join this or that country club, you'll have Fake Fun, and if you buy a designer handbag hoping to be the envy of everyone you meet, that is Fake Fun also.

If your dream was always to have a yacht, when you get one and it really is as wonderful as you dreamed, of course that will be real fun, not fake. If you love something, and you don't go after it because someone else told you to, you'll always have real fun, and never wonder why you bothered. If you are a big dork, in other words, you will always be having the real fun! So, yay. You'll be happy, and satisfied, because you won't care if the next guy's yacht is bigger. You just bought the one you loved, for yourself.

Americans love success, and well they should. You try for something, and then achieve it; abstractly that is a great thing. But now that the gap between rich and poor is the widest it has been since the 1920s, the whole concept of "success" needs more thought. The materially successful are now looking less and less successful according to long-held human standards of intelligence, competence, modesty and restraint. The fun they are having looks faker and faker. Consider the sad antics on view on Pajama Day at Google, reported by Jeffrey Toobin in *The New Yorker:*

> Pajama Day [...] happened to take place when I
> visited. (The event was to be madcap within reason;
> supervisors were told to convey the message that
> "pajamas means 'pajamas,' not 'what you sleep in.'")
> When I met with Sergey Brin, a co-founder of
> Google, he was wearing bright-blue p.j.s, with the
> company's logo stitched on the breast pocket [...]
> The most striking thing about Pajama Day at
> Google was how few people participated. Most of
> the rank and file saw the stunt for the manufactured
> fun that it was. They came to work in their usual

slacker uniforms of jeans and T-shirts—which are, in their way, as conformist as white shirts and ties were at I.B.M. in the nineteen-sixties.[63]

It's a scene straight out of Dunder Mifflin. I hope Google has its own version of *The Office's* Jim Halpert, maybe in Spiderman p.j.s, with his eyebrows slightly raised. (Is Sergey Brin in his personalized pajamas trying to show that he is a regular guy, and not a multi-billionaire corpocrat? Keepin' it real, as it were, in his specially-embroidered Google pajamas.)

Materialism, envy, "status anxiety", greed—all these things are based on a too-strong identification with what others think of us. It's bad enough that this unbalanced state of mind is so prevalent just with regard to the envy and unhappiness it creates. What is worse is that so many of us have become sundered from our own inner nature—have literally forgotten to consider what it is that would make us happy just on our own steam, just for ourselves. And have thereby rendered ourselves unable even to react to the outside world with authenticity or sense.

(Ťȟřȩȩ.)

Robert Frank is at pains to describe, in *Luxury Fever,* something I never even knew about: a watch that costs $3 million. Yes, a wristwatch, from Patek Philippe. You put it on your wrist! To tell the time. It's basically jewelry. Evidently they made four of these things, and each one cost more than the last, as in, there are more than four people who wanted one.

It's impossible to fathom that even one person would want to tell the time with this device, which to me looks more like a screaming $3 million insecurity machine. What is this thing supposed to do for you? It isn't going to make you any better looking! Isn't it kind of obvious that buying such a watch would be not only awful but impossibly gauche, when there are people in the world who are going to bed hungry? Meaning no disrespect to the engineers of Patek Philippe, who could probably devise a cold fusion machine, if they felt like it—when things have got to such a pass that you would seriously consider spending on (one!) watch enough money to keep, say, a few thousand starving people alive and in medicine for a year, it's nothing but clear that you have lost the thread.

Surely anybody would suppose these four guys to be far cooler and smarter if they would spend instead like $40,000 on a still-doubtless-presentable watch, and donate the other $2,960,000 to e.g. literacy programs, famine relief, medical aid to refugees, alternative fuel research, or a personalized wing of a university or hospital? And no, I don't care if they already did that with their other millions; surely they should do it again, with these—if what they want is to be cool.

Maybe it is pointless to bring up the possibility of a $3 million watch being just *wrong*—that is even perhaps a somewhat subtle question, but you would have to care about its being gauche or not, seeing how almost the only possible reason to buy such a thing would be to appear praiseworthy or enviable in some way to other people. There is nothing subtle about the gauche part. So if we think that these deranged moguls maybe ought to take it easy on the timepiece expenditure, it would be more practical to establish better metrics not for taxes, as Robert Frank suggested in 1999, but for coolness, like John Locke suggested in 1678:

> The principal spring from which the actions of men take their rise, the rule they conduct them by, and the end to which they direct them, seems to be credit and reputation, and that which at any rate they avoid, is in the greatest part shame and disgrace.
>
> [...] Where riches are in credit, knavery and injustice that produce them are not out of countenance, because, the state being got, esteem follows it, as in some countries the crown ennobles the blood. Where power, and not the good exercise of it, gives reputation, all the injustice, falsehood, violence, and oppression that attains that, goes for wisdom and ability. Where love of one's country is the thing in credit, there we shall see a race of brave Romans; and when being a favourite at court was the only thing in fashion, one may observe the same race of Romans all turned flatterers and informers. He, therefore, that would govern the world well had need consider rather what fashions he makes than what laws, and to bring anything into use, he need only give it reputation.[64]

૭ઌ

(F∅ṗṙ.)

Some years ago I met a spectacularly rich girl whose parents' house in Bel-Air was a temple to competitive consumption, the headquarters of a modern-day Trimalchio. It was like a house for giants, with vases in the foyer the size of phone booths, and a fireplace big enough to roast a brace of giraffes in. A really embarrassing and ostentatious place; I couldn't imagine anybody who wouldn't think that it was a horribly embarrassingly vulgarly showy place. So their middle-class guests like me are thinking, if I were this rich, I would never ever live like this. But you have to praise everything, because it is all so gaudy and it was all put there to be praised, especially by people like me, because you've been asked to dinner and it would be really bad form not to be kind. And kindness in surroundings like these, unfortunately, means fawning. If you're not fawning, you haven't gone the distance and will appear unappreciative, so the whole thing is a kind of a mess. Anyway at dinner, we got to talking about travel, and complaining about how uncomfortable it is to fly ten hours from LA to Europe, whence our host had only just returned. And, horror! it turned out she had been made to endure the indignity of flying commercial. She stared in real incomprehension when I said, "Shoot, even business class is wasted on me, I'm so short."

Few of us I daresay waste much time getting upset about the fact that we don't get to fly around in a G-V all day long. Nowadays that seems pretty wasteful, even just considering the amount of pollution one jet plane creates. Plus, you still have to go to the airport and endure however many hours of blah up there, no matter what kind of vehicle you're stuck in. How much can it really matter, seriously, what stupid airplane you are on? So long as it stays aloft and gets you to your darned destination, I mean.

If you are so bored or disaffected, and your life doesn't offer sufficient interest to you, so that you spend a lot of time dreaming about winning the lottery or some other weird thing that would render your current life totally obsolete, so that you would magically get a better one. I submit to you that swanning around in private aircraft is not going to fix you, not even the teensiest bit. Attracting the envy of others is not going to fix you; half the time it is fake to start with. Note how conformist types who have drunk that Kool-Aid become totally furious when we fail to envy them; we're depriving them of the fuel that gives them a sense of self. The whole thing is senseless, doomed.

If you embrace your dork nature, however, rich or poor, you will be able to zoom through life in a far happier frame of mind. The dork mentality is neutral regarding materialism *per se,* but it does protect every dork completely against the malady of *competitive* consumption, because no dork requires a feeling of superiority in order to achieve happiness. Dorks need and want the love, but they aren't about to give up their personal inclinations for it. By remaining true to their own real intellectual, spiritual and emotional imperatives, and balancing them with their natural desire for companionship and bonhomie, dorks are providing their lives with a center of purpose and meaning.

I'd like to stress that the need for a personal balance between inner- and other-directedness hasn't been addressed, at least not in the sociological works we studied in preparation for writing this book. *The Lonely Crowd*, the groundbreaking book by David Riesman that introduced the whole concept of inner- versus other-directedness, concentrated on mass social tendencies; it wasn't about individuals at all. That basic focus among serious students of the subject has continued until the present day. *No Logo* by Naomi Klein and Kalle Lasn's *Culture Jam* rage against the Evil Corporation; *Nation of Rebels* counsels us to dedicate ourselves to political activism; in *The Conquest of Cool*, Thomas Frank simply throws up his hands, exclaiming, "[T]he mass society critique was one with which American capitalism was singularly well prepared to deal—which is why it sometimes seems we will never be rid of it." The anti-consumerist bibles don't offer practical techniques for creating better cultural frameworks; often as not, they just advise us to smash the ones we have.

The imperative to live life differently keeps building until the day it breaks through the surface.

When it happened to me I was in my neighbourhood supermarket parking lot. I was plugging a coin into a shopping cart when it suddenly occurred to me just what a dope I was. [If only!—Ed.] *Here I was putting in my quarter for the privilege of spending money in a store I come to every week but hate, a sterile chain store that rarely carries any locally grown produce and always makes me stand in line to pay. And when I was finished shopping I'd have to take this cart back to the exact place their efficiency experts have decreed, and slide it back in with all the*

Flickr photo by ibay-daniel, creative commons

other carts, rehook it and push the red button to get my damn quarter back.

A little internal fuse blew. I stopped moving. I glanced around to make sure no one was watching. Then I reached for that big bent coin I'd been carrying in my pocket and I rammed it as hard as I could into the coin slot. And then with the lucky Buddha charm on my keyring I banged that coin in tight until it jammed. I didn't stop to analyze whether this was ethical or not - I just let my anger flow. And then I walked away from that supermarket and headed for the little fruit and vegetable store down the road. I felt more alive than I had in months.

—*Kalle Lasn,* Culture Jam

Kalle Lasn's first step as a "culture jammer"—wrecking the shopping-cart machine at his local supermarket—enraged, apparently, because they had no local produce!—had the sole and immediate effect of irritating the holy hell out of everyone who came after him and tried to get a shopping cart. *Culture Jam* is full of similarly "anarchic" suggestions for the rest of us; it's a would-be manifesto for a punk/art army of vandals that, of course, the author imagines himself leading. Good luck with that! In the meantime, we can shop at the "culture shop" that the noted anti-consumerist has got on his own website, Adbusters.org, and even buy his "cruelty-free" sneakers instead of the cruel Nike ones. I am not kidding. You can also hire his non-ad-agency ad agency, seriously—"if the cause is right."

Lasn, Klein and other well-known ragers-against-the-machine only address the potential answers to our problems in terms of mass movements—in their respective cases, again, movements they are visibly desperate to lead themselves. That kind of cultural criticism, we do not need. ("Follow me! Break things! Rebel! And then do whatever else I say do!" Oy.)

Alain de Botton in *Status Anxiety* recommends, in his half-hearted, Eeyoreish way, equal parts "bohemianism" and philosophy; his book, however flawed, represents something of a step forward from the Lasn perspective, because he looks to individuals to break their own chains, fashion their own worlds. By embracing the philosophical worldview, considering the brevity of life, understanding oneself to be "a speck on a speck on a speck"—de Botton argues that we will achieve a certain freedom from the materialist prison. But de Botton doesn't seem to realize that we will have a better shot at freedom if we embrace life, and not stifle ourselves in a lot of mournful ruminations on our impending death.

It's not the 19th century anymore, and it may be too late for the world to be changed with a book. Probably a good thing, too, given how the Marx business turned out. But de Botton is right up to this point: if we focus on the problem of competitive consumerism from the individual perspective—not by trying to form a movement—it is pretty easy to solve, and without wrecking even a single shopping-cart machine.

This is a matter of awareness, not activism or revolution. It's personal, not societal, not generational. It's the thing that can save anyone from the creeping consumerist malaise that has got all the pundit-knickers in such a twist. Are we not rich yet? Go outside. The blue vault of the sky above you will never be, can never be bigger or more beautiful than it is right now, which is to say eternally, mind-blowingly so, no matter how much money or which friends or what car you have or had or will have. The icy sweetness of ice cream can never taste better than it will today; how could it? Have you seen photographs of your great-grandparents? Have you ever been in love? Heard music, read a great novel? Most of what we need, we already have, if only we could learn to be aware and appreciative. Thomas Traherne, the 17th-c. author of the *Centuries of meditation,* made the same observation, in the following passage about the innocence of his own childhood:

> 'The Corn was Orient and Immortal Wheat
> which never should be reaped, nor was ever sown. I
> thought it had stood from Everlasting to Everlasting.
> The Dust and the Stones of the Street were as pre-
> cious as Gold. The Gates were at first the end of the

World, the Green Trees when I saw them first through the Gates Transported and Ravished me; their Sweetness and unusual Beauty made my heart to leap, and almost mad with Ecstasy, they were such strange and Wonderful Things; The Men! O what Venerable and Reverend Creatures did the Aged seem! Immortal Cherubims! And the young Men Glittering and Sparkling Angels and Maids strange Seraphic Pieces of Life and Beauty! Boys and Girles Tumbling in the Street and Playing, were moving Jewels. I knew not that they were born or should die...'[65]

Dorks are mocked for their appreciation of the "wrong" things, but really they are just alive to so much of the beauty that goes unseen by others. Beauty is in every moment, free to everyone.

If life is already beautiful, we won't ever feel insecure enough to be bullied into buying consumer products. We already have what they're trying to sell us—no, we already have so much more than the pathetic nonsense they are selling us. If we're really alive, we'll never need status, or wealth, or anything we can't find or create for ourselves. If we are free we won't need liberating. If we already know, we won't need to be told. And voilá, the Man's hold on us is broken.

Great Moments in Dorkismo, Vol. IV

Joseph Cornell: Dork-in-the-box

L'Egypte de Mlle Cléo de Mérode, photo via Webmuseum

This famously untrained artist lived with his overbearing mom and his ailing brother for almost his whole life on a street called Utopia Parkway in Nyack, New York. Cornell's intense shyness, his bizarre obsessions (ballerinas, opera singers, collecting old films, records and ephemera of all sorts, Dada and surrealism, making incredibly weird and beautiful assemblages, B movies), and his stubborn indifference to outside influence—classic dork attributes, all. It is the intense richness and exoticism of Cornell's inner world, its stark contrast to his relatively humdrum external one as a fabric salesman and mama's boy, that catapult him to the summit of the dorkistocracy. That, plus his absolute fidelity to his own strange and compelling vision. Cornell's real character was a lot like Steve Buscemi's fictional one in *Ghost World;* melancholic, alienated, catastrophic sex life, etc., but with deep glints of humor, beauty and excitement visible from the outside. So one gathers, at least, from reading what must be one of the very best biographies ever written about an artist: *Utopia Parkway* by Deborah Solomon.

Cornell made a famous film, *Rose Hobart,* which was a sort of art-mashup nineteen minutes long, made from a supposedly terrible jungle movie called *East of Borneo* and projected through a blue lens. This movie was shown in 1936 at the Museum of Modern Art; it's odd how this totally withdrawn guy was able to attract so much attention from the New York art world, but he was. Salvador Dali showed up at the screening of *Rose Hobart* and became either furiously jealous or just plain furious, and overturned the film projector.

Ťhe €řəd'e øf Døřkiſmø

(Øπe.)

Aye!

[Piano chords. **Hostess** (Chapman in drag) escorts **Old Ratbag** (Jones in drag) onto stage.]

Ghastly Quizmaster: Jolly good! Well now Madam your first question for the blow on the head this evening is: Which great opponent of Cartesian dualism resists the reduction of psychological phenome-

flickr photo by Steve Punter, creative commons

na to a physical state and insists there is no point of contact between the extended and the unextended?

Ratbag: I don't know that!

Ghastly Quizmaster: Well — have a guess!

Ratbag: Oh... Henri Bergson?

Ghastly Quizmaster: ...is the correct answer! (Piano chords)

Ratbag: Ooh, that was lucky. I never even heard of him.

Ghastly Quizmaster: Ha ha ha![66]

Gilbert and Sullivan, the Kinks, Spike Milligan, P.G. Wodehouse, Benny Hill, Bridget Jones, Reginald Perrin, Adrian Mole and Georgia Nicolson, and that august dork ensemble, Monty Python. Mirthful and yet serious, principled, but not stuck up, fabulously cool and totally lame, and not about to give up either thing for a minute; the whole world knows and loves that classic English flavor of dorkismo. If I were to detail examples of British dork heroes, this book would be a thousand pages long. We learned a lot of it from them.

Augustus Fink-Nottle is surely the most eminent of Wodehouse's august stable of dorks, famed for his obsession with newts and his undying love for the gloopy Madeline

Basset (even though Gussie eventually winds up eloping with Emerald Stoker, the American millionairess who has been posing as a cook at Totleigh Towers, after she makes him a steak and kidney pie.) So deep does the dork vein pulse through the British character that quite recently, *Observer* journalist Max Hastings saw fit to compare London's glamorous and unhinged mayor, Boris Johnson, to the aforementioned Fink-Nottle in the following terms: "[Johnson displays] a façade resembling that of PG Wodehouse's Gussie Finknottle [sic], allied to wit, charm, brilliance and startling flashes of instability."[67]

It's very, very difficult to imagine anyone in the U.S. press comparing Antonio Villaraigosa or Michael Bloomberg to a fictional newt enthusiast.

(Ťwǿ.)

Nay.

We Americans love the British, whether they are good guys or bad. We love a worldly English villain in the movies, as interpreted by George Sanders, Sean Bean, Jeremy Irons, and

Graffito in Graz from flickr photog southtyrolean

Gary Oldman; in literature, the bad British nobleman stretches from the 18th century all the way to *The Da Vinci Code*. And a sophisticated English good guy is better still—the Saint, Napoleon Solo and James Bond are loved as much or more here than they are in their native land. Why is this? In part it's because the British are viewed as both worldly, and capable; worthy adversaries and worthy friends; powerful forces, for good and for evil.

Certainly Americans have got the "cultural cringe" of colonials vis-à-vis the mother ship, though that term was coined by and on behalf of the similarly situated Australians. Our relatively brief history and necessarily lesser achievements create a sense of inexperience, innocence and even inferiority. The English seem to have long known something that we still don't. There's the consistent excellence of their myriad contributions to the sciences, medicine, literature, philosophy, law, politics, architecture, design, music. Their venerable universities and museums, their churches, their cultural and professional institutions. Their wonderful bravery and heroism in the second war.

And finally, there is the perfect foil to their refined aesthetic, intellectual and moral standards, their stoicism and restraint: the time-honored British tradition of refusing to take anything too seriously. A sort of understanding that there is a time for putting away everything to do with *comme il faut*. So it is very, very upsetting to see that of all people the Brits should begin to adopt, as they recently seem to have done, the vulgar, shallow materialism they have rightly been castigating in Americans for about forever.

The English, those heroes of the Enlightenment, who

managed now and then to improve the lot of their far-flung subjects, who accepted Indian independence with grace and no bloodshed, who laid the groundwork for so many of the political advances of the 20th century—how is it that they have dropped the 21st-c. ball? Whither the modesty, frugality, self-deprecation, hard work, humor, restraint and unstoppable intellectual curiosity, and the fuck-you elegance of their perennially shabby clothes and furnishings? Where are they now, these far-sighted men and women?

One place they are super not is in the pages of *How To Spend It,* the seething mash-note to conspicuous consumption that defiles the *Financial Times* every Saturday morning.

Now, I mainly love the *Financial Times* (founded 1888.) Their crossword compiler Cinephile, an 85-y.o. vicar and high-toned wag, is a dork of the first water. But just a few peachy pages away from Cinephile comes the big glossy monstrosity that is *How to Spend It* (founded 1980,) full of unpleasant-looking, skeletal women in the ghastliest rags imaginable, and page after page of wealth-worship and brainless self-congratulation so cluelessly snotty that it makes *Vanity Fair* look like *Index on Censorship.*

This issue on my desk is called, "Life, Liberty and the Pursuit of Golf", and features a lush photo of the new Liberty National golf course ("joining fee," half a million US$.) Inside, there's an ad for the Rolex Cup, a sailing contest: "The Rolex Cup is as much about prestige, glamour and beauty as it is competition." Photo of Oyster Perpetual Yacht-Master (a watch.) On to the lead article, about how rich Chinese are snaffling up all the Bordeaux. Massive pull quote: "They only drink 100-point Parker wines. I know someone whose everyday wine is Château Petrus." Gleeful, Faginesque British wine merchant: "The Chinese believe that the most expensive wine is the best. That makes it a very interesting market in which to do business."

"In the Maldives there are now more yoga teachers, Pilates instructors and life coaches per square mile than you'll find even in London's Notting Hill," which would apparently be a recommendation, from "Travelista" Sophy Roberts. A Jaeger-LeCoultre watch the size of your head, floating inexplicably above guys playing polo on futuristic skyscraper-rooftop (whoa, Nelly!)

In "Memphis Bella", collectors with "an allergy to safe good taste", no kidding, are advised to stock up on scary "madcap" 80s-style Italian furniture too idiotic to appear in the apartments of Pepe Le Pew; at Hospes Hotels, a bored vapid chick stands vapidly around in a marble hallway, with caption, "I won't settle for the look, I seek the pulse"; if she means her own pulse, god it's like shooting fish in a barrel.

"Last winter just 500 skiers found their way to Kashmir's Mount Apharwat," which at least conjures an image of zillionaires lost in Himalayan crags. "Stuff from the States is rarely stylish," sniffs tech guru Jonathan Margolis; "Motorola phones only 'got' design a couple of years ago." He is a weird guy. "Why don't people love Bose?" he asks. "Is it that slightly bovine name?"

Suddenly, leaping around in the forest, a fantastically mean-looking chick in Bela Lugosi makeup and a $2200

Gucci dress is irritably brandishing a $1600 Prada attaché. Later, stunned probably from having been banged on the head with a brick by an irate reader, she returns in a black silk corset and a huge ribbed stiff collar reminiscent of those x-ray bibs at the dentist, except covered with gold beads ($250—seems cheap, suddenly—at Harvey Nichols.) Cufflinks in the form of tiny diamond-studded pistols would once have elicited a snort of derision from any Englishman worthy of the name, because nobody but an American would be so ludicrously flash, and yet … here they are.

Even the crassest Yank going (Graydon Carter?) would have some trouble with materialism this coarse. We had to import the likes of Anna Wintour to achieve anything like the same thing here.

Reggie Nadelson is American, but she lives in London. And in her "How to Spend It" column "Consuming Passions," she advises readers of conscience to bathe in asses' milk or champagne ("and make it the good stuff") as a conservation move (to save water, ha ha!) "Oh, and in glass from Venini in Venice." It is true that in the 18th century Lord Hervey *et al.* bathed in and drank asses' milk, for their complexions, for which they were hilariously crucified by Alexander Pope. And milk has got alpha-hydroxy acids in it, so this was actually not such a bad idea. But even in Alexander Pope's time they did not attempt to bathe in a Venetian vase, and they were satisfied with regular asses' milk, and did not demand a top brand. Oh, god. What I am trying to say is that this woman is incoherent, and it seems to be catching. "Americans outside New York are, of course, unspeakable." Hey, she ought to know.

But the worst is saved for last, literally the last page's

"Perfect Weekend" column, because how on earth can the guy currently in charge of the National Gallery be the slightest bit interested in telling the public about his exercise regimen, or where he buys corduroy trousers, or cheese?[68] It's the absolute antithesis of everything we admire about England, it's a total betrayal of dorkismo. Only imagine Kenneth Clark doing such a thing! How John Lennon would have laughed, if anybody had asked him where he bought cheese!

When will we realize that a list of shops doth not a character make?

One cannot entirely blame this hapless guy for his participation in the cult of celebrity that dominates life in the Man's world. It's the water we're swimming in, where it's natural for a survey of some poor curator's consumer preferences to appear in the newspaper, alongside a photo of him looking like a smug, bescarfed high-school French teacher. This can't be good for the National Gallery, can it? It's a dignified British institution, it stands for scholarship and passion and history, right? So is the whole National Gallery totally cringing right now? Is it?

Let us pray, dork faithful, that somewhere in England the heirs of Monty Python are taking all this stuff down, and will show no mercy.

Three

Yeah, Yeah, Yeah

The Beatles were always having fun, or trying to. They were rebellious, but not bitter like Dylan or Lenny Bruce (at least, not at first;) they were elegant, but in an antic way, without any model-faced posing like the Stones and their crashingly boring Satanic Majesties. They noodled about in the snow in outlandish outfits and claimed to wish to be an octopus, they starred in a psychedelic cartoon and had lovely things to say about the Monkees (John Lennon said, "The Monkees? They've got their own scene, and I won't send them down for it. You try a weekly television show and see if you can manage one *half* as good.") Lennon in particular made a whole way of life out of flippancy and playfulness, and was much misunderstood in the classic dork manner. He was the very picture of a man who could "be himself, and not care what anyone thinks," and the result was often a complete train-wreck. When his lonely-sounding interview with Maureen Cleave was published in the *Evening Standard* in 1966, the most terrific PR mess in rock and roll history was unleashed. Lennon had said: "Christianity will go. It will vanish and shrink. I needn't argue about that. I'm right and I will be proved right. We're more popular than Jesus now. I don't know which will go first—rock 'n' roll or Christianity."[69]

Lennon was 25 years old at that point, and a dyed-in-the-

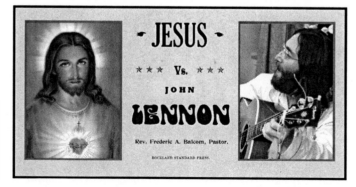

wool absurdist, and what he meant was, largely: how insane is this, the Beatles are more popular than Jesus now. In 1966, of course, that was only an incontrovertible, if weird, fact. Lennon's oblique praise of Jesus in the same interview went unnoticed ("Jesus was all right but his disciples were thick and ordinary. It's them twisting it that ruins it for me.") As for "them twisting it," next thing you know, the Beatles were banned in South Africa, and a radio station in Texas staged a public burning of their records.

However, there was a wonderful attempt among the dorkier clergy to rescue Lennon from this pitchfork-waving mob. *The New York Times* reported the comments of Reverend Richard Pritchard, a Presbyterian minister from Madison, Wisconsin: "There is much validity in what Lennon said. To many people today, the golf course is also more popular than Jesus Christ."[70] From the dorky fastnesses of Canada, the Right Reverend Robert Kenneth Maguire remarked, "I wouldn't be surprised if The Beatles actually were more popular than Jesus. In the only popularity poll in Jesus' time, he came out second best to Barabbas."[71] (This Bishop Maguire was such a cool guy, over and above the huge dorkismo. He left all his $3 million fortune to a foundation for homeless youth, except for a trust he set up for retired clergy in the Diocese of Montreal, so that each receives a $100 gift at Christmas.)[72]

Bless the Beatles and their invincibly cheeky grace, maybe the most blissfully dorky thing ever to come out of that scepter'd isle.

5uch ə'løøfneʃʃ +ø əll vμlgəř cəřeʃ

Who can describe the charm of love? That conviction that we have found the being who was destined by nature to be ours, that sudden illumination of life, that new value attacking to the slightest circumstances, those swift hours, the details of which elude us in retrospect through their very sweetness, leaving in our mind only a long trail of happiness; that playful gaiety which occasionally mingles for no reason with our general feeling of tenderness; in our love's presence such pleasure, in her absence such hope; such aloofness to all vulgar cares, such feeling of superiority towards all our surroundings and of certainty that, on the plane on which we are living, society can no longer touch us; and that mutual understanding which divines each thought and responds to each emotion—the charm of love! Those who have known the charm of love cannot describe it!

BENJAMIN CONSTANT, *Adolphe*

M. and I met because of the sadistic 10th-grade trig teacher Mr. Brose, who objected to me coming in late and stoned out of my gourd every day and basically dangling out of the windows goggling at this blond Ultimate Frisbee knockout bizarrely named Courtney Severyn III. Brose's idea of discipline included baiting me with stuffed rats in the communal homework folder, trying to persuade me to touch some kind of electric shock device straight out of *Dr. Who,* and eventually making me sit next to the perfectly-behaved, bespectacled black-haired snow-white ultra-dork at the front-and-center desk: M. Erf! I was thinking, such a well-known hopeless geek was he. I can still remember the first whiff of musk, his very characteristic, intimate natural scent and thinking like oh, man. Soon enough I would be burying my face in his clothes for ages with eyes closed, breathing.

He said, is that David Bowie you are writing the lyrics to on your folder, in such miniscule script. I am ashamed to say that I responded, in a voice dripping with adolescent incredulity, "*You* know who *David Bowie* is?!" When I was the one who didn't know anything. I did not know how beautifully M. could play the piano, upon which he would shortly be composing songs in my unworthy honor. How he would be able to make me howl with laughter, with a single microscopic lift of one thick black eyebrow.

To love a dork is to become the sworn protector of the beloved's individuality and freedom, no matter what. Conversely, once you have really been free with someone, once you've really been known and embraced for your true dork self, even once, you would never go back. My allegiance to M. was (and is, come to that) so absolute that it encompassed the acceptance and even defense of many, many things I can't stand, including Joni Mitchell, Birkenstocks, vegetarianism and Samuel Richardson. Because M. loved those things, they acquired a new grace in my eyes. Even when I couldn't begin to see for myself what he saw in them, I could never mock them in quite the same way again, so much did I love and respect the brilliantly gifted composer of such inimitable works (coming thick and fast, in those halcyon days,) as "O, to be a Slow-Moving Sloth?"

> *O to be a slow-moving Sloth!*
> *O for a life that's free!*
> *O to be a slow-moving Sloth,*
> *And spend my whole life*
> *Asleep in a tree!*

In return, I was free to share with M. everything down to the dorkiest detail. He might roll his eyes at my obsession with Todd Rundgren, or tease me about the slender literary merits of *Naked Lunch* or *The Fan Man,* but his censure did not extend to me. I bathed in the welcoming glow of sympathy and did not fear to introduce my sudden enthusiasms for

Fantasia or cheongsams or Maslow's Hierarchy of Needs. Because of M. I developed the dork-adapted eye, so that I never considered another companion again except in light of how free we might be together.

I was so lucky, you will agree. But even

David Bowie bei Rock am Ring 1987, Elmar J. Lordeman via Wikimedia Commons

back then I was no longer on the lookout for Prince Charming. I had been inoculated against that whole business at the age of six, having fallen catastrophically in love with this angelic blond Dorian Gray Jr. aged seven, whose name was Jeff Broadmoor (decades on I can still picture him really clearly; he looked something like the young David Sylvian.) He did not care for me in the least, and was infatuated instead with the buck-toothed, ponyish (and, admittedly, very pretty and nice) Teri. I apprehended dimly that he didn't like me in quite the way he liked her; but, I think, I lived on crumbs of hope (for what?! I had no idea) until we lined up one fateful day after lunch, boys in little pressed chinos and short-sleeved shirts, girls in little candy-colored a-line dresses, white bobby socks and patent-leather Mary Janes, to go back into the classroom. Without warning the god of my whole tiny existence drew near me with a purposeful look, like an avalanche of snow-cold blond, blue-eyed beauty bearing down on me. The blood began to pound in my head, my chest; my breath stopped; he reached out his hand, so gently; it came near my face, and deftly he plucked a single hair from my head, thereby paralyzing me, and the whole of the earth. Then he went up to Teri, and did just the same to her! It was astonishing! I am still astonished. Then, he rubbed Teri's single long, auburn hair on his velvety white cheek and said, "This is a Teri hair. Mmmmm. And this," he continued disdainfully, "is a Maria hair. Ew yuck, yuck!" and threw my sad little besotted hair on the ground.

I was so surprised! I'd had no idea he found me repulsive, nor even that he'd had the faintest clue that I liked him so much. I would have supposed that he didn't know that I existed, even. How come not the hair of some other hapless female?! I still don't know, but I can tell you that it was a whole incredible, instantaneous education. That peak moment where your beloved approaches you for the first time. The heart-stopping vertigo, the lightning-awakening skin, etc. etc. 100% fully functional, age six. And I somehow knew this, completely knew this dangerous thing for what it was, respected its potential toxicity, its power to unmoor, to unman. Or, ungirl, rather. The way he mocked me was so brutal, though, that a crossroads appeared before me, almost visibly. I could (a) die, or (b) see that whatever it was I was going to be needing from boys, this cruel and beautiful creature was never ever going to be in a position to provide. Surface beauty no longer appeared to me as anything more than itself, after that one instant, couldn't be trusted for its own sake. Maybe it was then that I started thinking about the possible existence of something more complex than physical perfection, something beneath the skin to love—to the point where eventually, a person's imperfections became the thing that interested me most.

That the embrace of imperfection is the quintessence of love and understanding is an old idea, as venerable as the equally valuable idea that imperfection is itself precious, and extends all the way through creation. Francis Bacon said: "There is no excellent beauty, that hath not some strangeness in the proportion."

Even in the case of the coolest person in the world (David Bowie, as we were getting round to saying earlier,) it's his imperfections that made us love him most. Had his incisors not been kind of weirdly protuberant, had he not come from Brixton and begun his career as a folk singer and even trained as a mime, had he not looked but too hopeless in his pointy outer-space shoulder pads, what then? Love doesn't gloss over idiosyncrasies and even defects; it practically demands them. Love thrives on particularity and unconventionality; the personal, not the public. Without a little *folie*, no *folie à deux*.

There was a very lovely example of this at a performance of Charles Ross's *One-Man Star Wars Trilogy* at Lamb's Theatre off-Broadway. Which is just a fantastic show, by the bye, in case it ever comes back.

In stark contrast to the consciousness of superiority and discernment that people feel when they attend e.g. a Tom Stoppard play, most of the patrons at the *One-Man Star Wars Trilogy* were visibly embarrassed to be there. But their excitement was nearly uncontrollable, and there was nothing blasé about them; there were only maybe sixty or eighty people in the audience, but every single one was full of pep. There was a gang of six teenage girls, nearly 67% of them wearing glasses. Maybe ten families, each containing a little boy or two, one of whom was sporting his own Boba Fett helmet. My own demographic—goofy, dangerously giddy-looking brunettes, each with a long-suffering boyfriend in tow—four brace. Two extra-wide beer-drinking-looking guys with shaved heads, trying to act all macho, but unable to conceal the radiance of their *Star Wars* excitement. And then, the most wonderful duo: a brainy-looking fag hag of regulation chubbiness, beautifully dressed, with super-carefully-applied makeup on her lily-pale skin, and her willowy young man; and they were yapping about theatre, theatre theatre. Where they'd sat in this and that orchestra section, how each performer had fared in this show and that. It was tough to make out their exact words, though I was trying desperately. But suddenly I heard his lilting voice quite clearly, confiding to her in the sweetest tone: "Well… *our* definition of 'good' is rather different!"

"Our definition of 'good'"!! Ours alone! O god, I *loved* that, because they were really happy, happy in this way that no one could ever touch. Their innocent camaraderie had completely, effortlessly—permanently—smashed all the vile fictions perpetrated on innocent people by the Man, just by their spontaneity and intimacy. They shared not quite like lovers, nor like friends, nor "mates"—but like souls.

The Man will try to keep you from having anything like this. There's only one kind of intimacy the Man has got on offer. The only one, one and only, the divine one who can make you feel happy to be alive—okay, fine, but the mass-market True Love doesn't really know a thing about you, and doesn't have to. You'll fall in love at first sight. He'll pour you a Bacardi Somethingorother, or see you driving your new Mitsubishi, and you'll both just *know*. It won't be for any particular reason, it will just happen. But it will be perfect always. Because true love, don't forget, is like heaven. You need only your lover to be complete and whole. He is divine, like an angel, he is your whole world and more, and it will be like this forever and ever and ever. (Can we point out that this is so hopelessly false, and what is more, you wouldn't like it if it *were* true. Now, here is a horrible stew of freakish delusions concocted in order to enslave you and make you buy shampoo! We like to think we've gotten past fairytales but in truth, many of us are more in thrall to them than ever. What was *Sex in the City* but Cinderella in a pair of tedious Manolo Blahnik shoes?)

According to the Man, there is just one handsome prince or beautiful princess out there for you, so he or she has got to be amply provided with all the fixin's. The mundane details here are all taken care of via a prefabricated list of clues by which True Love may be recognized. These are trotted out in practically every commercial, every magazine ad, every billboard. The True Love is muscular and virile, and ridiculously rich, driving his sports car just a little too fast (ha, ha!), or else a lissome nymph, just a little too young for you and tricked out in skin-baring Euro-togs, attracting all eyes as you stroll into the nightclub. It's *Pretty Woman*, basically, a thoroughly stale and exhausted tableau. There will be flowers, fawning sommeliers, jewels, holidays in the Caribbean. So desirable is your True Love that you have sex about six times a day (Viagra can help!)

What Do You Want From Life?

—The Tubes

That well-known literary form, the Personal Ad, is a type of poem devoted to these vain, senseless fantasies:

DROP DEAD GORGEOUS
Single woman, 34, 5'7, 115, degreed, bright, great
sense of humor, 34-24-34 seeking SWM, 35-55 for

marriage. Please be affluent, educated, attractive, generous.

It's weirdly impossible to form an image of an actual person based on the above (it's from an old *LA Weekly*,) in spite of all the measurements and things. The most you could say is that anyone who would ask a stranger to "please be affluent" with a straight face seems utterly unlikely to have a "great sense of humor," an indifferent sense of humor, or half a dozen functioning synapses. And don't think it's the enforced brevity that's to blame. The personal ads published in the *London Review of Books,* the Alfred A. Knopf of the personal-ad genre, have offered the following prospects:

> Tap-dancing Classics lecturer. Chilling isn't it? Box no. XXX

> Love is Strange - Wait till you see my feet. Box no. XXX

Let us now praise dorky men.

A column inch in the *LRB* is ample room for the sketch of a delightful wag whom I bet any man to 45 would like to date:

Woman, 38. WLTM man to 45 who doesn't name his genitals after

German chancellors. You know who you are and, no, I don't want to meet either Bismarck, Bethmann Hollweg, or Prince Chlodwig zu Hohenlohe-Schillingsfürst, however admirable the independence he gave to secretaries of state may have been. Box no. XXX[73]

Young people in all their fear of unworthiness of an as-yet-unknown intimacy are particularly susceptible to falling for the big lie, here, spending frantic hours at the gym and buying quack skin creams for their nonexistent wrinkles. Where instead, they could be looking for a companion with whom to construct an impregnable dork fortress, like this one:

My boyfriend is a dork. Despite the fact that I'm continually amazed by the extent of his dorkiness, he's kind of a cool dork, and I'd like him to continue being my boyfriend. Because of this, I've sacrificed much of my own coolness to acclimate myself to the dork subculture. In time, I've come to tolerate and sometimes even enjoy dorky staples like online comic strips, anime and Adult Swim.

I'm lying. I still can't tolerate anime.

By far, the hardest thing to get used to was the hours upon hours spent using a chunk of plastic and some cords to make a little guy on TV fight with other little guys on TV. For most people lacking a Y chromosome, everything about video games is confusing, from the plotline to the controllers to why it was necessary to skip all classes the day "Halo 2" came out.

[...]

[W]atch out - entire weekends can disappear in a game-induced stupor. When I got my boyfriend "Fable," I became so engrossed in its intricate plot-line (my character could barter, go fishing, get married and kill wasps with an iron katana) that the only task I accomplished for an entire week was finding the 20 silver keys necessary to obtain the Murren Greathammer.

When I finally found it, I wept with joy. And then I slapped myself.[74]

Yay! No—I mean wait, don't slap yourself! But Yay. Her character could "barter, go fishing, get married and kill wasps with an iron katana" (oh, man!—a dorkier list of accomplishments than which can scarcely be imagined. Haha!)

He stood at the Xerox machine, copying long passages of Kant. The machine was piled high with his books. He wore a light cotton shirt and baggy white pants. He turned to say hello, scooped up his nickels from the copier and put them into his pocket. The coins slid down his leg and rang when they spilled out on the floor by his shoes. He blushed. He was definitely my kind of guy.

From *The 100th Boyfriend*, ed. Bridget Daly and Janet Skeels (Seattle: Real Comet Press, 1987.)

Ťheiř ðøřk məteřiəlʃ

'Be happy for this moment. This moment is your life.'
OMAR KHAYYAM

Jane Eyre: An Autobiography was published in 1847, and caused an immediate sensation. England wracked its brains trying to figure out who the mysterious "editor" Currer Bell might be—a man?—a woman? (The adamantine balls—a man! The romance, the longing—a woman, surely?) And was this Currer Bell of low, or high station?—impossible to tell, since Bell frankly exhibited the sensual, even lustful sentiments of a peasant (as the Victorians reckoned such matters, at least in public,) as well as the unmistakably erudite, articulate manner of not only a scholar, but a gentleman.

JANE EYRE.

An Autobiography.

EDITED BY
CURRER BELL.

IN THREE VOLUMES.
VOL. I.

LONDON:
SMITH, ELDER, AND CO., CORNHILL.
1847.

Title page of the first edition of Jane Eyre. via Wikipedia.

In fact Charlotte Brontë (to give Mr. Bell his real name) was then living in genteel squalor with her utterly messed-up whacked-out brother, her two brilliant novelist sisters and their tyrannical father in a freezing, remote vicarage in Yorkshire, where it was pretty easy to go incognito for a while after the novel's publication (and easier still to contract every type of hellacious respiratory malady, a variety of which bore off all three of her surviving siblings not long after the publication of *Jane Eyre*.)

Jane Eyre is a novel about a young woman without prospects, without wealth, beauty, or connections, but with fire enough to power a dozen Victorian governesses. Her ambition is to find love, acceptance, and her own place in the world, and as the novel progresses it becomes clear that she will accept nothing less. No-one and nothing can ever deter *Jane Eyre* from what she knows to be her own right path, nor ever make her feel small, or low; she's magnificently brave and exciting in every moment of her deservedly immortal story; she is supremely, imperially, eternally herself.

This rare book consequently speaks to the deepest part of the reader, should he permit himself to be touched there. Can he identify with the heart of a small, poor girl of limited means and untamed character? And later, once the author's identity became known—could he sympathize with a story, written by the obscure daughter of a country parson, that so many had denounced as coarse, unwomanly and unchristian? The answer, even in the mid-19th century, was very often a resounding Yes. *The Atlas* described *Jane Eyre* as "a book to make the pulses gallop and the heart beat, and to fill the eyes with tears," and their noble reviewer did not lack for company, the most amiable of whom may well have been W.G. Clark, who wrote in 1849 that he "took up *Jane Eyre* one winter's evening ... sternly resolved to be as critical as Croker,"[75] but found that "as we read on we forgot both commendations and criticism, identified ourselves with Jane in all her troubles, and finally married Mr. Rochester about four in the morning."[76]

Charlotte Brontë did not invent the extraordinary person of Jane Eyre so much as fashion her straight from the materials of her own voluminous mind and heart. Critics will argue forever about how much of the author found its way into the

The Brontë sisters Anne, Emily and Charlotte, painted by their total mess of a drug-addict brother, Branwell (who appears as a kind of ghost, third from the left.)

heroine; such complex, subtle connections are difficult to unravel, but in this case one of the threads is free and clear. Brontë's biographer, the great novelist Elizabeth Gaskell, describes a conversation that once took place between the three sisters:

> [Charlotte] once told her sisters that they were wrong—even morally wrong—in making their heroines beautiful as a matter of course. They replied that it was impossible to make a heroine interesting on any other terms. Her answer was, 'I will prove to you that you are wrong; I will show you a heroine as plain and small as myself, who shall be as interesting as any of yours.'[77]

Even morally wrong—what was moral, what was necessary, was to show the extraordinary in a real person, not an idealized one. She really did it, too, both in her own life, and in Jane Eyre's. Not for nothing do we call England the Cradle of Dorkismo!

This bit of literary history, though, gratifying as it is, is only an introduction to the point I wish to make, which is this: there is a genius blogger named Lan Yinzhong, the most extraordinary Chinese girl of 19, who recently wrote a very beautiful post, "Bing Jane Eyre;" and because Miss Lan has articulated the concluding arguments of this book far better than I ever could, I will leave it to her to make them in an excerpt here.

The great thing about "Bing Jane Eyre" is that a Chinese teenager, who is on the face of it just about as far from being a nineteenth-century Yorkshire clergyman's daughter as it is possible to be, *completely gets this book* in the most thrilling way. In fact, she gets it better than many, many of Brontë's contemporaries did. *Jane Eyre* was widely condemned by conservative contemporary critics who found the novel too rough and too sexy, or as one of them put it, brimming with the "grosser and more animal portion of our nature."

Elizabeth Rigby, later Lady Eastlake, biggest cow ever

Chief among these was Eliza Rigby, the Grundiest Mrs. Grundy you ever saw, who reviewed *Jane Eyre* for the *Quarterly Review* in 1848. Horrible as she was, there is a certain truth to her description of the subject novel:

> Altogether the autobiography of Jane Eyre is preeminently an anti-Christian composition. There is throughout it a murmuring against the comforts of the rich and against the privations of the poor, which, as far as each individual is concerned, is a murmuring against God's appointment—there is a proud and perpetual assertion of the rights of man, for which we find no authority either in God's word

or in God's providence—there is that pervading tone of ungodly discontent which is at once the most prominent and the most subtle evil which the law and the pulpit, which all civilized society in fact, has at the present day to contend with. We do not hesitate to say that the tone of mind and thought which has overthrown authority and violated every code human and divine abroad, and fostered Chartism and rebellion at home is the same which has also written *Jane Eyre*.[78]

No doubt! If by "Christian" we mean the conventional I-got-mine "morality" of the Victorian moneyed classes, as distinct from the actual teachings of Jesus Christ—those wicked Chartists were trying to expand voting rights and obtain more democratic representation in Parliament, after all!!—well then yes, Mrs. Rigby-Grundy was absolutely right. As for "God's appointment" of rich and poor … it's quite true, *Jane Eyre* is proudly and perpetually against that idea, and does indeed share something of the defiant spirit that had overthrown the monarchy in France. The novel's backbone is a wild exhortation against inequality.

Which, I might add, is just like the backbone of this book.

I was talking with this very nice boy once, just a random conversation in some random shop—a video store, I think—about pizza. Like (I believe) most people, I am extremely fond of pizza, and I made this point by observing that even if they were to put, say, strawberry yogurt on it, I would probably still eat it.

"Oh, man," he replied feelingly. "I'm livin' in that same world." That was such a pleasing phrase, I thought.

If we think of human beings, of ourselves, as livin' in that same world not only as regards pizza, but in a more general sense, as being essentially equal to one another; constituted alike, and possessed of the same potential—then we will never spend even a moment trying to be superior to the next guy. We won't be "too good" for this or that. We won't be yapping about "God's word" or anyone else's being *against* the rights of man, either. We will only be interested in seeking out common ground with our fellows, to the best of our ability. The author of "Bing Jane Eyre" is just such an evolved creature, possessed of exactly this inclusive spirit.

Bing Jane Eyre

Book review of Jane Eyre

I have read *Jane Eyre* many times in Chinese. And every time I read, I always appreciate this great woman. Well, I know Jane, the woman who is the main character of the book is really ordinary person, ordinary looking, ordinary family and ordinary learning. But I never think her of ordinary.

First part of the book, Jane was adopted by her uncle. But her uncle died early, so her aunt kept on raising her. Generally speaking, a girl at the age of 10 would be quiet and lovely, and would obey what the adults told her. But if she was, she was not Jane Eyre. Her aunt was cruel to her and always locked her up in a red-room without noticing her crying. In such a poor circumstance, she grew up with strong. [...] When she left her aunt's house, she once said, "I will never call you aunt again as long as I live, I will never come to see you when I am grown up." But when her aunt was going to die, she went to see her immediately. But unfortunately, up to her death, Mrs Reed had not showed penitence. Jane said at last "Love me, then, or hate me, as you will. You have my full and free forgiveness: ask now for God's and be at peace." It is easy to hate someone, but very hard to forgive. I'd really appreciate Jane with such a great moral character. To say I mercy you is easy, but what if with your really heart.

[...]

When [Jane] knew that Mr Rochester was engaged, she thought she must leave. She did not want to be a mistress though she loved Mr Rochester. What she said that time was so brilliant and full of her eagerness to be equal and free. "Do you think, because I am poor, obscure, plain, and little, I am soulless and heartless? You think wrong!—I have as much soul as you—and full as much heart! And if God had gifted me with some beauty and much wealth, I should have made it as hard for you to leave me, as it is now for me to leave you. I am not talking to you now through the medium of custom, conventionalities, nor even of mortal flesh; it is my spirit that addresses your spirit just as if both had passed through the grave, and we stood at God's feet, equal—as we are!"

> We are all equal, aren't we? No matter where we are born, who we are, at God's feet, we are equal. Through Jane Eyre, Charlotte express what most women wished, to change their social position, to be treated free and equal.
>
> Being Jane Eyre, in other words, are we all Jane Eyres? We are not all beautiful, smart, but we can have spirit. Our soul are different and have own color. We can all become Jane Eyre.[79]

That I find the slightly unorthodox English in this essay enchanting, I have already implied. This is not because of any quaintness, or out of a desire to mock—on the contrary, Miss Lan's mastery of English is a lifetime away from mine of Chinese—but in pure admiration, because in the written language of a non-native speaker it is possible to see the mind reaching for a thought more directly; for the thought itself, rather than for a constructed or conventional pose. In the case of this author, whose thought is not only so noble and true, but is also positively bursting with a fiery dork passion, this absence of any veil of compositional formality is a thousand kinds of awesome.

Great civilizations from Periclean Athens to the United States were precariously built on the dawning belief that every human being is of equal value. Democracy, cultural pluralism, loving thy neighbor as thyself—"Life, liberty and the pursuit of happiness"—as citizens, as humanists, and in our spiritual lives, this is the central organizing principle of human progress. Everyone will one day be free to pursue his own vision of the good life, whether that means dressing up as Mr. Spock, seeking professional advancement or making a piece of toast for breakfast. That is the ideal we live by, even right now, in this country. Right?

Well, even conceiving of such a thing as "high" and "low" culture, of "cool" and "uncool," directly contradicts this principle. Scratch the surface of the phrase "high culture," and you will see that it is a direct descendant of the idea that some of us are literally worth more than others, "appointed by God" or whatever—but that idea is false, false, false. The truth is that we are all human, and all of equal worth.

Dorks throughout history have helped, are still helping, to lay down the foundation of this ultimately unshakable doctrine. Lesser souls, frightened, weak and self-conscious, have sometimes tried to push us away from the path of equality, but always there are a few total dorks to lead us back again. Because no matter what happens, we can use what we know to try to connect with each other, rather than trying to smash one another down out of insecurity or fear. The power and permanence of this idea comes from the fact that it is true. It always comes back to us, because it's *true.* Our soul are different and have own color. Human beings are equal, and equally valuable.

All three, or four (or five) of us authoresses are livin' in that same world, too, separated by however many hundreds of years and thousands of miles, and all have written to the same purpose—Jane Eyre, Charlotte Brontë and Currer Bell, myself and the author of "Bing Jane Eyre" are all of us asking the same thing: be yourself. Don't be scared. Love yourself, and love the world. Go on, just get out there.

Test Your Dork-Q

INSTRUCTIONS.
Please note: there's a web version of the quiz with automatic scoring at http://www.dorkismo.com/dork.html.

To take the quiz, please mark the circle corresponding most closely with your position on each question. They are not super logical, completely polar opposites, so if you agree equally (or at different times) with both options, mark one of the central circles. It is like a magazine quiz, not very scientific! (p.s. don't read the Scoring page following this one before taking the quiz, or it will mess up your results.)

1. My parents are horribly embarrassing.	O O O O O O	My parents are awesome.
2. I love talking about taboo subjects.	O O O O O O	I clam up in the presence of controversy.
3. Meeting new people scares me.	O O O O O O	Is it hot in here, or is it just you?
4. I like a bit of intoxicants in a social situation.	O O O O O O	I'd better hang on to what little sanity I have left.
5. I want love.	O O O O O O	And I'll do whatever it takes to get it.
6. I want to be envied.	O O O O O O	I don't care what other people think.
7. I'm in love with my car.	O O O O O O	I dream of driving a super-fabulous vehicle, like the Batmobile, or a Ferrari.
8. Conventionality scares me.	O O O O O O	I can pass for square, when I have to.
9. I am unique.	O O O O O O	I'm a lot like other people.
10. I feel comfortable around "normal" people.	O O O O O O	And who the hell would that be?
11. Astrology is cool.	O O O O O O	Astrology is bogus.
12. My friends are the coolest people ever to live.	O O O O O O	My friends are too hopeless.
13. I plan to divide by mitosis.	O O O O O O	I am looking forward to grandchildren someday—or, I have them already!
14. I love expensive things.	O O O O O O	I love getting a deal.
15. Why can't we all just get along?	O O O O O O	Some people need to be schooled, and in the worst way.
16. I have a sneaking fondness for seeing the bad guy get a huge comeuppance.	O O O O O O	I don't want to know about any bad guys.
17. This gorgeous specimen walks into the room; I wonder what this person is like.	O O O O O O	I am going to try to get some of that.
18. I love to keep up on trends by reading Star Magazine.	O O O O O O	I love to keep up on trends by reading the newspaper.
19. I love going out.	O O O O O O	I love staying home.

Scoring.

In order to calculate your score, count your results according to the table below, from left to right:.

1. 6-1	6. 6-1	11. dummy question	16. 6-1
2. 1-6	7. dummy question	12. 6-1	17. 6-1
3. 6-1	8. 1-6	13. dummy question	18. dummy question
4. 6-1	9. 1-6	14. 6-1	19. 6-1
5. 6-1	10. 6-1	15. 1-6	

Now add all your scores together; you'll have a number between 15 and 90. That is your raw dork-Q score. You can check your result against the Pyramid of Human Felicity on the next page.

Dorkismo advances the argument that a healthy human being balances reasonable concern about what others think of him with deeply-held personal convictions that cannot be altered from the outside. This balance can be expressed in colloquial terms as a kind of midpoint between narcissism and misanthropy. The balanced mind is a dorky mind, indicative of someone who isn't scared of looking like an idiot, and who will cheerfully indulge his own eccentricities and those of others in an unprejudiced, inclusive way.

A high degree of dorkismo is an effective weapon against the evils of modern society—competitive consumerism, political and philosophical apathy, solipsism and alienation.

Dork-q is a casual measurement of this balance. The quiz is designed to fake you out to a certain degree; of the nineteen questions, only fifteen are scored. The others are just to throw you off the scent of what qualities are being measured, in order to ensure casual, honest responses. Likewise a central point between the loosely-conceived poles is omitted in order to protect against 'center bias'.

A "perfect" score, indicative of a mind in balance between concerns of "fitting in" and a knee-jerk rejection of the opinion of one's fellow men, is in the 52-53 range. If your score falls very much above 58, this is suggestive of a tendency to worry too much about what others think of you, and you might consider throwing your weight around a bit more, and about developing more confidence in your own ideas and aims. If you are much below 47 or so, this may be indicative of a certain degree of misanthropy, an instinctive mistrust or dislike of your fellow-man. It's possible that you might enjoy the company of others, if you gave them a chance to get to know you; that you might be happier if you were to become more interested in, and accepting of, your fellows.

The Pyramid of Human Felicity.

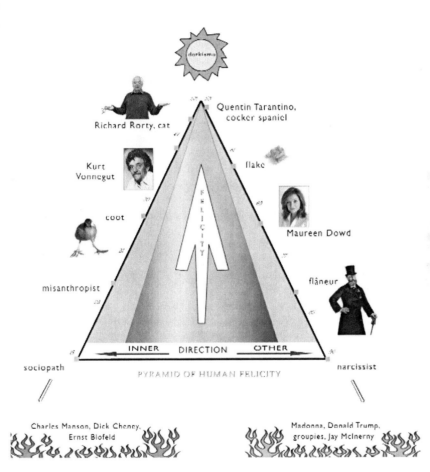

dorkismo

Richard Rorty, cat

Quentin Tarantino, cocker spaniel

Kurt Vonnegut

flake

coot

FELICITY

Maureen Dowd

misanthropist

flâneur

INNER   DIRECTION   OTHER

sociopath

PYRAMID OF HUMAN FELICITY

narcissist

Charles Manson, Dick Cheney, Ernst Blofeld

Madonna, Donald Trump, groupies, Jay McInerny

Bibliography

Allen, Woody. "The Metterling Lists," collected in *Getting Even.* New York: Random House, 1971.

Baldwin, James. "The Black Boy Looks at the White Boy." *Esquire,* May 1961.

Ballard, J.G. *A User's Guide to the Millenium.* London: Harper Collins, 1996.

Birkerts, Sven. "Critical Condition," *Bookforum,* Spring 2004.

Biskind, Peter. *Easy Riders, Raging Bulls.* New York: Simon & Schuster, 1998.

Botsford, Gardner. *A Life of Privilege, Mostly.* NY: St. Martin's Press, 2003.

Carey, Peter. *Wrong about Japan.* New York: Knopf, 2005.

de Botton, Alain. *Status Anxiety.* London: Hamish Hamilton, 2004.

Ebert, Roger. *Robert Ebert's Movie Yearbook 2005.* Kansas City, MO: Andrews McMeel Publishing, 2004.

Frank, Robert. *Luxury Fever.* New York: Free Press, 1999.

Frank, Thomas. *The Conquest of Cool.* Chicago: University of Chicago Press, 1997.

Friedman, Rick. *The Beatles. Words Without Music.* New York: Grosset & Dunlap. 1968.

Gans, Herbert J. *Popular Culture and High Culture.* New York: Basic Books, 1974.

Gaskell, Elizabeth. *The Life of Charlotte Brontë.* London: Penguin Books, 1997.

Gibson, William. *Idoru.* New York: G. P. Putnam's Sons, 1996.

Gopnik, Adam. "The Power Critic," *The New Yorker,* March 16, 1998.

Greenberg, Clement. "Avant-Garde and Kitsch." *Partisan Review,* Fall 1939.

Heath, Joseph, and Potter, Andrew. *Nation of Rebels.* New York: HarperBusiness, 2004.

Jacobs, Norman. *Culture for the Millions? Mass Media in Modern Society.* Princeton, NJ: D. Van Nostrand Co., Inc., 1959.

Klein, Naomi. *No Logo.* Toronto: Knopf Canada, 2000.

Larsen, Stephen and Larsen, Robin: *A Fire in the Mind: The Life of Joseph Campbell.* Rochester, VT: Inner Traditions, 2002.

Lasn, Kalle. *Culture Jam.* New York: William Morrow, 1999.

Mailer, Norman. "The White Negro: Superficial Reflections on the Hipster." Reprinted in *Advertisements for Myself.* New York: G.P. Putnam's Sons, 1959.

Marx, Gary T. "The White Negro and the Negro White." *In Phylon.* Summer 1967, vol.28, no. 2, pp. 168-177.

Michie, Elsie B., editor. *Charlotte Brontë's Jane Eyre: A Casebook.* Oxford: Oxford University Press, 2006.

Portman, Frank. *King Dork.* New York: Delacorte Press, 2006.

Remnick, David, et al. *The Complete New Yorker.* New York: Random House, 2005.

Riesman, David et al. *The Lonely Crowd.* New Haven: Yale University Press, abridged ed. with new foreword, 1961.

Rigby, Elizabeth. "Vanity Fair—and Jane Eyre," *Quarterly Review* 84:167, December 1848.

Rorty, Richard. *Contingency, Irony, and Solidarity.* Cambridge: Cambridge University Press, 1989.

Rose, David. *They Call Me Naughty Lola : Personal Ads from the London Review of Books.* New York: Scribner, 2006.

Sontag, Susan. "Notes on 'Camp'." *Partisan Review,* Fall 1964 Volume XXXI, Number 4.

Traherne, Thomas. *Centuries of Meditations.* Bertram Dobell, editor. London: Bertram Dobell, 1908.

Toobin, Jeffrey. "Google's Moon Shot," *The New Yorker,* February 5, 2007.

Vreeland, Diana. *D.V.* New York: Knopf, 1984.

Wallace, David Foster. "E Unibus Pluram." *The Review of Contemporary Fiction,* Summer 1993, collected in *A Supposedly Fun Thing I'll Never Do Again.* Boston: Little, Brown, 1997.

Whyte, William Hollingsworth. *The organization man.* Philadelphia: University of Pennsylvania Press, 2002.

Wolcott, James. "Dwight Macdonald at 100," *The New York Times,* April 16, 2006.

Notes

[1] Urbandictionary.com is of particular interest here, because anyone on the Internet can go along and vote on the relative accuracy of the definitions of slang words, all of which are likewise submitted by the Internet-surfing public. Consequently the mood of the general public (or at least, as much of that public as

uses the Internet) can be gauged very effectively using the results published on the site. Citations compiled 7/1/2005.

[2] George Orwell, "Good Bad Books," via WebLiterature, http://www.webliterature.net/literature/Orwell/WL11259/BK11.html

[3] Lev Grossmann, "The Quest for Cool," *Time,* September 8, 2003.

[4] J.G. Ballard, *A User's Guide to the Millennium* (London: Harper Collins, 1996), 14.

[5] Peter Biskind, *Easy Riders, Raging Bulls* (New York: Simon & Schuster, 1998), passim.

[6] Quoted in Peter Biskind, *Easy Riders, Raging Bulls.*

[7] Stephen and Robin Larsen: *A Fire in the Mind: The Life of Joseph Campbell* (Rochester, VT: Inner Traditions, 2002), 541.

[8] BBC News, 17 February 2003

[9] Via http://www.natalieportman.com/npcom.php?page_number=116

[10] Via http://www.cultureisnotoptional.com/discuss/viewtopic.php?t=692&sid=3daf53cee93177d138fd3c63354f36e2

[11] Via http://www.interbit.com/blogger/2003_12_07_archive.html

[12] Via http://www.comixfan.com/xfan/forums/printthread.php?t=22892&page=3&pp=20

[13] Eric Zorn, "Camera phones' spy potential not a pretty picture," *Chicago Tribune,* October 28, 2003.

[14] Eric Zorn, "In end, solution to 'slob' debate proves easy call," *Chicago Tribune,* January 1, 2004.

[15] Trainspotting is a hobby where you hang around waiting for trains, and then when one comes, you write the serial number of the train in a little book. It's like birdwatching, only it's trains, and yes, people really do this.

[16] Lawrence, "The Origins of 'Otaku'", *Cornell Japanese Animation Society,* November 4, 2003, via http://www.cjas.org/~leng/otaku-origin.htm

[17] Maggie Jones, "Shutting Themselves In," *The New York Times,* January 15, 2006.

[18] Which, at the time of this writing, can be seen in HD on crunchyroll.com.

[19] 2channel, the chat system where the real story of Densha Otoko took place, is the biggest Internet forum in the world, and is hugely popular in Japan. Nearly all the posts on 2channel are anonymous, and there is no moderation at all. The closest American equivalent to 2channel might be something like Usenet or the Well, or the old Prodigy bulletin boards, in the Internet's earliest days.

[20] Thomas Frank, *The Conquest of Cool* (Chicago: University of Chicago Press, 1997).

[21] James Baldwin, "The Black Boy looks at the White Boy," *Esquire,* May 1961.

[22] Norman Mailer, "The White Negro: Superficial Reflections on the Hipster," reprinted in *Advertisements for Myself* (New York: G.P. Putnam's sons, 1959), passim.

[23] Thomas Frank, *The Conquest of Cool* (Chicago: University of Chicago Press, 1997), 12.

[24] Gary T. Marx, "The White Negro and the Negro White" *Phylon,* Summer 1967, vol.28, no. 2, pp. 168-177.

[25] Edward Shils, "Panel Discussion" in Jacobs, *Culture for the Millions?* (and yeah it is really called that), 1959.

[26] Susan Sontag, "Notes on 'Camp'," *Partisan Review,* Fall 1964 Volume XXXI, Number 4, passim.

[27] David D. Kirkpatrick, "Winfrey Rescinds Offer to Author for Guest Appearance," *The New York Times,* October 24, 2001, passim.

[28] Chris Lehmann, "Jonathan Franzen: A Defense," *Slate,* November 1, 2001, via http://www.slate.com/id/2058036/entry/2058061/

[29] Heidi Julavits, "Rejoice! Believe! Be Strong and Read Hard!" *Believer,* March 2003, passim.

[30] Via http://www.gawker.com/news/todo/todo-cormac-mccarthys-blood-meridian-215341.php

[31] Richard Rorty, *Contingency, Irony, and Solidarity* (Cambridge: Cambridge University Press, 1989), 73.

[32] David Foster Wallace, E Unibus Pluram, *The Review of Contemporary Fiction*, Summer 1993, passim.

[33] "In Memoriam: David Foster Wallace 1962–2008," via http://www.pomona.edu/adwr/president/dfw2.shtml

[34] Ibid.

[35] Clement Greenberg, "Avant-Garde and Kitsch," *Partisan Review,* Fall 1939.

[36] Adam Gopnik, "The Power Critic," T*he New Yorker,* March 16, 1998.

[37] Sven Birkerts, "Critical Condition," *Bookforum* Spring 2004, via http://www.bookforum.com/archive/spr_04/birkerts.html

[38] James Wolcott, "Dwight Macdonald at 100," *The New York Times,* April 16, 2006.

[39] Clement Greenberg, "Avant-Garde and Kitsch," *Partisan Review,* Fall 1939.

[40] John McCarten, "The Current Cinema," *The New Yorker,* collected in The Complete New Yorker, passim.

[41] Gardner Botsford, A Life of Privilege, Mostly (NY: St. Martin's Press, 2003).

[42] Variety, December 2, 1942, via http://www.variety.com

[43] Via http://www.amazon.com/gp/cdp/member-reviews/A2XU3B96Q95L3S

[44] Richard Schickel, "Darkest Woody," *Time*, Monday, August 7, 1978.

[45] in "Everything you always wanted to know about sex* *But were afraid to ask," 1973.

[46] Woody Allen, "The Metterling Lists," collected in *Getting Even* (New York: Random House, 1971).

[47] Geoff Andrew, "Woody Allen," *The Guardian,* September

27, 2001, passim.

48 http://www.gofugyourself.com

49 "Big Fug," *Go Fug Yourself,* via http://gofugyourself.celebuzz.com/go_fug_yourself/2006/06/big-fug.html

50 Brooks Barnes, "Fashion Trash Talk Is a Big Blog Hit For the 'Fug Girls,'" *The Wall Street Journal,* September 28, 2005, via http://online.wsj.com/public/article/SB112786877952654094-kHrKoA6FtsxOzDUhbPswT87g9pY_20051028.html?mod=blogs

51 Heath and Potter, *Nation of Rebels* (New York: HarperBusiness, 2004), 125.

52 Lewis Hyde, *The Andy Warhol Foundation for the Visual Arts, Paper Series on the Arts, Culture, and Society, Paper No. 8,* Created Commons 1998.

53 Toby Young, *How to Lose Friends and Alienate People* (Cambridge: Da Capo Press, 2002), passim.

54 Ibid.

55 Heath and Potter, *Nation of Rebels* (New York: HarperBusiness, 2004), 124.

56 Diana Vreeland, *D.V.* (New York: Knopf, 1984).

57 Malcolm Gladwell, "The Coolhunt," *The New Yorker,* March 17, 1997.

58 Thomas Frank, *The Conquest of Cool* (Chicago: University of Chicago Press, 1997), 198.

59 Gladwell, op.cit.

60 Grant McCracken, "Who Killed the Cool Hunter?" via http://www.cultureby.com/trilogy/2006/06/who_killed_the_.html; citing Lev Grossman, "The Quest for Cool," *Time,* September 8, 2003

61 Gladwell, op.cit.

62 Robert Frank, *Luxury Fever* (New York: Free Press, 1999), passim.

63 Jeffrey Toobin, "Google's Moon Shot," *The New Yorker,* February 5, 2007.

[64] John Locke, "Reputation," *Locke: Political Essays,* ed. Mark Goldie (Cambridge: Cambridge University Press, 1997), 271.

[65] Thomas Traherne, *Centuries of Meditations,* ed. Bertram Dobell (London: Bertram Dobell, 1908), 158.

[66] Monty Python, "The Attila the Hun Show," via http://www.intriguing.com/mp/_scripts/braincel.php

[67] Max Hastings, "Boris the buffoon is dead. Stand by for Boris the mayor," via http://www.guardian.co.uk/commentisfree /2008/mar/30/boris.livingstone, March 30, 2008.

[68] One place he buys cheese at is Verde's, "Jeanette Winterson's delicatessen," apparently.

[69] Maureen Cleave, "How Does a Beatle Live? John Lennon Lives Like This," *London Evening Standard,* March 4, 1966.

[70] *The New York Times,* August 6, 1966.

[71] Rick Friedman, *The Beatles. Words Without Music* (New York: Grosset & Dunlap. 1968), 33.

[72] "Bishop Robert Kenneth Maguire: Reaching out to help those in need in a significant way," *Entrust,* via http://www.loftcs.org/acrobat_pdfs/entrust.pdf

[73] David Rose, *They Call Me Naughty Lola: Personal Ads from the London Review of Books* (New York: Scribner, 2006).

[74] Jaci Boydston in Kansas State Collegian, quoted in "Video Game v. Girlfriend," via http://www.chocolatepizzastilettolove .com/2006/12/video-girlfriend.html

[75] That would be John Wilson Croker, an Anglo-Irish states-man and author also called the "human death-watch beetle," the most feared and loathed literary critic of his times.

[76] Quoted in *Charlotte Brontë's Jane Eyre: A Casebook,* ed. Elsie B. Michie (Oxford University Press, 2006), 25.

[77] Elizabeth Gaskell, *The Life of Charlotte Brontë* (London: Penguin Books, 1997).

[78] Elizabeth Rigby, "Vanity Fair—and Jane Eyre,"*Quarterly Review* 84:167 (December 1848), 153-185.

[79] Lan Yinzhong, "Bing Jane Eyre," November 6, 2008, via http://hi.baidu.com/rememberblue/blog/item/82e5ca01c8cfe7047 38da5aa.html

Photo Credits

Back cover photo by Olaf Gradin, whose spectacular cosplay photos may be also be seen at http://www.gradin.com/photos (reprinted here by permission, and via flickr creative commons.)

Photos of David Foster Wallace by Steve Rhodes (flickr.com/photos/ari/), used with permission.

Acknowledgments

Thanks to Richard Johnson, Albert Johns, Leigh Anne Jones, Michael Mullen, Erwin Hösi, Prabhakar Ragde, Marcus Gray, Diana Hoffer, Christina Wilson, Ken Smoker, Dean Costello, Amina Sanchez, Michael Jolkowski, Carol Delucia, Steve Rhodes, Jeff Falco, Harm Tron, Jason Preston, Jeff Boscole, Christie Mellor, Richard Goldman, Amanda Peppe, Toni Devito, Sherry Virbila, Patty Clark, Mary MacVean, Daniela Roveda, Jody Labov, Celeste Wesson, Anna Sones, Kristin Herbert, Steven Mikulan, Sandra Ross, Kateri Butler, wallace-l, Jordan Ellenberg, Dan Crane, Frank Portman, Kate Kasserman, Richard Cunningham, Melissa Conway, S.F. Winser, Chuck Paone, Teresa Zampino and Marie Mundaca: dorks one and all.

LaVergne, TN USA
09 March 2010
175387LV00001B/34/P